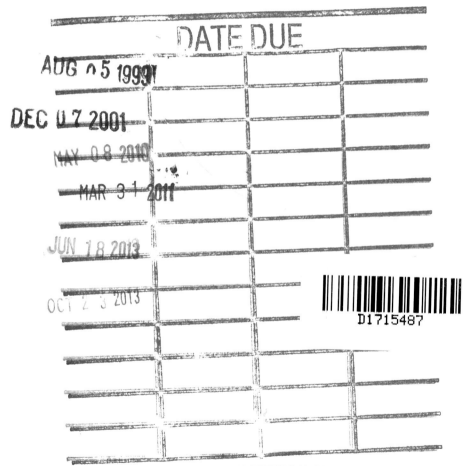

Street Gangs

Yesterday and Today

Other Books by James Haskins

Diary of a Harlem Schoolteacher
Resistance: Profiles in Nonviolence
Revolutionaries: Agents of Change
The War and the Protest: Vietnam
Profiles in Black Power
A Piece of the Power: Four Black Mayors
From Lew Alcindor to Kareem Abdul Jabbar
Religions
The Psychology of Black Language
    With Hugh F. Butts, M.D.
Deep Like the Rivers: A Biography of Langston Hughes
Black Manifesto for Education—Editor
Jokes From Black Folks
Adam Clayton Powell: The Man and His Times
P.B.S. Pinchback: A Biography
Jobs in Business and Office
Witchcraft, Mysticism and Magic in the Black World

Street Gangs
Yesterday and Today

By JAMES HASKINS

Illustrated with prints and photographs

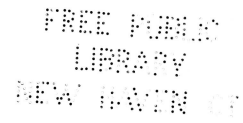
HASTINGS HOUSE, PUBLISHERS,

NEW YORK

To Ruth Ann

Second printing, July 1975

Library of Congress Cataloging in Publication Data

Haskins, James, 1941–
   Street gangs: yesterday and today.

   SUMMARY: A history of street gangs from colonial times to the present discussing why they have persisted, who joins them, what needs they satisfy, and what they have in common with establishment groups.
   Bibliography: p.
   1. Gangs—United States—History—Juvenile literature. [1. Gangs—History] I. Title.
HV6439.U5H35   301.18′5   74-1375
ISBN 0-8038-2662-1

Published simultaneously in Canada by
Saunders of Toronto, Ltd., Don Mills, Ontario

Printed in the United States of America

The photographs on pages 118, 119 and 120, reproduced by permission of Holt, Rinehart and Winston, Inc., are from *The Vice Lords: Warriors of the Streets* by R. Lincoln Keiser. Copyright © 1969 by Holt, Rinehart and Winston, Inc.

CONTENTS

Introduction   7

Street gangs in history   13

Street gangs in the modern era   77

Bibliography   141

Glossary   145
   Slang of early gangs
   Slang of modern gangs

Index   151

INTRODUCTION

Young—as young as twelve, not much older than twenty-one or twenty-two. Black—or Puerto Rican—or Cuban—or Mexican, depending upon the area of the country, but most of all, non-white. Urban—because, after all, the cities are the disease of America. Arrogant—because their parents are on welfare and they feel the world owes them a living, too. Cruel—hurting innocent people "just for kicks." Boot-wearing, jive-talking, gun-toting, finger-snapping, jacket-sporting groups of ghetto dwellers who adopt alarming or pretentious names for themselves and whose exploits, glorified by reporters and broadcasters, make respectable citizens uncomfortable, if not downright afraid. These are the characteristics most outsiders would list if asked to define *gangs*.

It might be hard for them to accept the idea that today's urban ghetto street gang has roots that extend deep into the soil of America, much deeper than the layer of earth that is the twentieth century. It might be hard for them to accept the idea that nearly every nationality is represented in American gang history. And it might be hard for them to accept the idea that, basically, a gang is a group, sharing common characteristics with other groups in America.

Originally, the word gang had no negative meanings. In old English, *gang* simply meant "a going together." A gang was a number of people who went around together, in other words, a group. Perhaps, in our modern era, the negative meaning for gang was invented by those who did not belong to the group that went around together, although they most assuredly belonged to, or made haste to form, groups of their own.

Man is by nature a joiner. From earliest history until the present time the group, though it has become increasingly complex, specialized and diversified, has remained a basic social unit among human beings. A group can be as simple as three inseparable friends, as important as a community, and as powerful as a giant industrial conglomerate, yet all share certain basic elements: unity, identity, loyalty, reward.

The reasons for man's desire to form groups are most easily seen in adolescent peer groups. Any teenager, and anyone who remembers what it was like to be a teenager, knows about the dawning sense of independence, the desire to break away from the family or from whatever adult authority exists and to find one's own identity separate from that authority. Although in adolescence, identity is defined by one's peer group almost as much as it is defined by the family or other adult authority, there *is* a difference. After all, the teenager chooses the friends he wishes to be with, usually because the identity he seeks is similar to the identity sought by them. Together, the members of the group further evolve a common identity, which can range from inventing a secret language, wearing similar clothing and other harmless acts, to stealing, vandalism or fighting. What kind of identity the members of the group seek, what kind of activity they engage in to achieve that identity, and whether they will eventually leave their adolescent peer groups to join similar adult peer groups depends in large measure upon class and in lesser measure upon sex. In general, it has been lower-economic-class males who have engaged in the kinds of activities that would define their groups as *gangs*, as we use the term today, although females have always been present to some extent in gang history.

What are the circumstances of low socio-economic class life that foster gang activity? There have been many studies on this subject, and their conclusions have ranged from weaker family ties to lack of communication between the sexes; but the most basic circumstance is that the poor have many fewer paths to "being somebody" open to them than do those of other classes. A poor person does not have to be very old before he realizes that in the eyes of the rest of the world he is a "nobody" or worse. Participation in gang activities is one way of feeling like "somebody". Identity, a sense of belonging, a sense of importance— for many in the lower economic classes gang activity has seemed the only way to fulfill these very important needs. This has been true, in urban centers across the United States, throughout its history.

Gangs are, and always have been, essentially an urban phenomenon. In this regard, the "outsiders" are correct, but their reason—"the cities are the disease of America"—is too simplistic. City life just adds another dimension to the sense of being "nobody" that people of lower economic classes feel. This other dimension—and it can be felt by city dwellers of every class—is loneliness.

Loneliness is most extreme in areas where tens of thousands of people live. A city person comes into contact with thousands of people every day; he knows only a handful. The others are nameless and unknown to him. On the other hand, he is nameless and unknown to them. He is "a foreigner," as psychotherapist Rollo May puts it, "pushed on and off the subway by tens of thousands of other anonymous foreigners." This loneliness is a tragedy in itself. Add to it the sense of being nobody that discrimination and poverty cause the poor to feel, and the result is often the urban street gang and the violent behavior with which it is associated.

This book includes accounts of apparently motiveless violent acts committed by street gang members. Outsiders, and, indeed, gang members themselves say they commit these acts "just for kicks," but there is an explanation beyond this. These kinds of violent acts by street gangs are a natural product of the combination of loneliness and "nobodiness,"—the complete anonymity—which street gang members feel. In his book, *Love and Will,* Rollo May explains how such feelings can lead to violent behavior:

> "The mood of the anonymous person is, if I cannot affect or touch anybody, I can at least shock you into some feeling, force you into some passion through wounds and pain; I shall at least make sure we both feel something, and I shall force you to see me and know that I also am here! Many a child or adolescent has forced the group to take cognizance of him by destructive behavior; and though he is condemned, at least the community notices him. To be actively hated is almost as good as to be actively liked; it breaks down the utterly unbearable situation of anonymity and aloneness."

This history of street gangs tends to focus on New York City, for New York City exemplifies many urban areas with gang problems. In addition, the book examines particular gangs. It does not and cannot mention every gang; those treated were chosen because they are typical, or especially interesting.

Hopefully, this book will help place today's street gangs in the context of history for the reader, and show that gangs are certainly not a twentieth century phenomenon. Also, it is hoped that this book will bring about a greater understanding of street gangs as a predictable result of America's greatest shame, the urban ghetto.

The gang was a family to all street cats. The gang fed him, gave him initiative, responsibility, and respect, which the system didn't give him because he was born poor. Born poor, you dig? Not just black. You got Puerto Ricans, Chinese, and poor whites who tell the same story.

—A NATION OF LORDS
by David Dawley

Bandit's Roost—the notorious den of nineteenth century gangs.
The Jacob A. Riis Collection, Museum of the City of New York

Gangs
in history

Street gangs may seem as contemporary as the morning headlines—one more symptom of the deterioration of urban life. But the street gang is no new phenomenon. Its roots extend deep into America's past. And the conditions that breed street gangs today are identical to those that have existed in America from the time it first took its place among nations.

A gang can be defined today in four basic ways. One, it is an organized group with a recognized leader and usually, less powerful lieutenants under his command. Two, it is a unified group, which remains together during peaceful times as well as during times of conflict (in contrast to a mob, which may unite in a riot but whose members go their separate ways when the rioting is over). Three, it shows this unity in obvious ways, such as wearing the same jackets or speaking a special language. Four, its activities are either criminal or somehow threatening to the larger society.

No groups completely fitting this description really existed in America until the early 1800's, but almost from the beginning of the European settlement of America there was gang-like activity. And as soon as strong class distinctions came into being it became possible for gangs to exist.

When Europeans first came to America they were little concerned with class structure or status. Their main concern was staying alive; their dream was a better life than the one they had left behind. The first settlers came mainly from England and the Netherlands, where most of them had been poor and belonged to the lower classes. In their native lands, they had faced a gloomy future of no inheritance, no property, and no possible chance of bettering their status. With very few exceptions, a peasant was doomed to be a peasant all his life. There were no "rags to riches" or "poor boy makes good" success stories. A peasant had very few choices. He could rent a run-down cabin and do paid labor, or work other people's land, or travel to London or Paris or Amsterdam to find work. But usually the only opportunity a peasant could find was through crime. He could become a pickpocket in the city, or he could join the bands of rogues and vagabonds who thronged the roads of seventeenth and eighteenth century Europe.

With the colonization of North America, a new alternative presented itself—a chance to start afresh, to throw off class distinctions, a chance to have land in a country in which there was room for all of Europe and then some.

Hopeful settlers flocked to America. But once they arrived, they found they could not be completely independent, for they owed allegiance and very often their living to merchants or colonization companies or wealthy Europeans whose lands they farmed or whose supplies they purchased.

Many of these first settlers did not succeed in staying alive, and before long there was a rather large number of orphans for the settlements to care for. While the settlements were still small, neighbors and friends took in the orphans and reared them as their own, or communities established orphanages. When the boys reached the age of 12 or 13 or 14, they were apprenticed to craftsmen in order to learn a trade; the girls became household helpers. They could not join the community as equals for many years, so these maturing orphans became a separate class in themselves.

Craftsmen and apprentices at work in an eighteenth century workshop.
New York Public Library Picture Collection

The ideal of the apprenticeship arrangement stressed mutual help and responsibilities—a family relationship, the master teaching his apprentice a particular craft and providing for his basic needs in exchange for the work and loyalty of the apprentice. Most apprenticeship arrangements, however, fell far short of the ideal. The master often stressed labor more than learning, trying to get as much work out of his apprentice as possible and paying little attention to the lad's needs. The apprentice, sensing that his work was considered of far greater value than himself, used work as a weapon—slacking off or damaging costly materials. As time went on the apprenticeship arrangement lost most of its family aspects, resulting in a group of alienated boys and young men.

The lads and wenches met when they wished, they drank rum at the taverns and they danced together till late in the night. Reproved, they threatened to burn the town down over the ears of the burghers. From time to time, disorderly gatherings and even open riots showed the limits of control. Apprentices were often among the active elements in the eighteenth century mobs.[1]

This situation worsened as settlements grew and took on the characteristics of cities. Some people were able to better their circumstances greatly. Many others were not so lucky. Urbanization made possible the growth of a class of servants, orphans and derelicts for whom nobody felt responsibility. In 1660, New York (which was then a Dutch colony called New Amsterdam) had a population of only 1000. Yet there was an orphanage and a poorhouse and everyone was provided for. By 1776, English New York had spawned a group of young, homeless boys who nightly were a source of trouble to respectable citizens.

Philip Montresor, a leading citizen of the day, recorded in his diary entry for January 14, 1766, . . . "children nightly trampouze the streets with lanthorns upon Poles and hallowing . . . the Magistry either approve of it, or do not dare to suppress it." [2] Already there was crime in New York streets and a concerned, respectable citizenry impatient with the authorities. But apparently, there was better communication between the concerned citizens and the authorities at that time, for on February 6th of the same year, Montresor writes, relieved, "This night several Children were dispersed by the watchman (for the 1st time) for parading the streets with 3 effigies and candles, being about 300 boys. Cryers and newsmongers and carriers . . ." [3] Montresor dates the event everlastingly—any concerned citizen who would consider 300 boys parading the streets with effigies as "several Children" could not be of a recent century! Yet youth "gangs" were not so much a problem as an annoyance in Philip Montresor's time, which was, after all, before the birth of America as a nation.

[1] Oscar Handlin and Mary F. Handlin, *Facing Life: Youth and the Family in American History*. Boston: Little, Brown & Co., 1971, p. 32.
[2] I.N. Phelps Stokes, *The Iconography of Manhattan Island*, Vol. V. New York: Robert H. Dodd, 1915, p. 760.
[3] Ibid., p. 761.

Older groups of criminals were, however, a real problem by this time. The busy port cities along the eastern seaboard attracted all manner of criminal types—pirates, sailors who had jumped ship, derelicts, drunks, pickpockets, cargo thieves. Although they usually worked individually or in pairs, groups of criminals also banded together, particularly pirates and cargo thieves.

By the time Philip Montresor had written the above-mentioned entries in his diary, Britain was imposing stiff and unfair taxes upon the goods brought into the colonies, and smuggling was a very profitable business. Groups of smugglers were active in the coastal towns, and although many colonists must have applauded them for foiling the British, most of the pirates were not motivated by patriotism. Black market prices for smuggled goods, although below the prices of taxed British goods, still allowed for a healthy profit. Certain groups of smugglers operated for years, and had they adopted names and a more distinct organization they would have been smuggling *gangs*.

Although the colonists were rightfully enraged against the British, many of the riots and disorders which took place in the years before the Revolution were not carried out by idealistic patriots. Hatred of the wealthy, arrogant British rulers and governors far out-weighed any clear dream of a new, independent country. Today, we like to see these disorders as examples of the colonists' hunger for liberty, but we have glossed over the true history of the pre-war agitators. Just as George Washington was continually troubled by troop desertions and just as the horrible winter of Valley Forge was due mainly to the refusal of farmers to give food to the Continental Army and to the refusal of the Colonies to give money or supplies, the citizen uprisings against the British were controlled by mob emotionalism, the excitement and adventure of being against authority, and the ordinary resentment between the "haves" and the "have-nots." Groups of men and boys delighted in starting or joining these riots and disorders and in the arson and looting that often followed.

A mob of colonists protest the Stamp Act.   *Library of Congress*

One Boston man, Ebenezer MacIntosh, was responsible for many pre-Revolutionary disruptions and in a later time might have been a gang leader. He commanded the allegiance of a group of South Enders, notorious for overwhelming Boston's North End mob in the bloody free-for-all that marked the annual Pope's Day celebration. But after some conversations with the Sons of Liberty, MacIntosh began to use his strength to protest the hated Stamp Act, which taxed printed documents—wills, deeds, even newspapers. In a series of violent protests, MacIntosh and a mob of rioters wrecked and looted the homes of various government officials. Though he was finally arrested, MacIntosh had become such a powerful figure that his release was immediately guaranteed by the threat of yet another riot.

After war was declared, the cities were in an almost constant state of turmoil, whether threatened by the British or not. City populations increased greatly, with either Loyalist or Patriot refugees swarming in to seek safety, depending upon whether the city was sympathetic to the British or the Revolution. In every city, criminals took advantage of the turmoil, but generally the attitude was "every man for himself," rather than a collective, gang-like spirit. The individualism of Americans at this time was not only confined to those who obeyed the law.

The end of the Revolutionary War and the American victory over the British did not bring about an end to the turmoil in the colonies. If anything, there was more unrest, for in driving out the British the colonists had also driven out the British government, police forces and other institutions of authority that were necessary to maintain an orderly society. A new government and new police forces took time to organize and begin to work. The cities, especially, saw more violence and mob activity involving former apprentices and orphans who had left their country villages for the excitement of the cities. In 1791 in Philadelphia, the editor of Dunlap's *American Daily Advertiser* complained bitterly about the seeming permissiveness towards the crowds of adolescents who nightly roamed the streets:

> The custom of permitting boys to ramble about the streets by night is productive of the most serious and alarming consequences to their morals. Assembled in corners, and concealed from every eye, they can securely indulge themselves in mischief of every kind. The older ones train up the younger, in the same path, which they themselves pursue; and here produce in miniature, that mischief, which is produced, on a larger scale, by permitting prisoners to associate together in crowds within the walls of a jail. What avails it to spend the public money in erecting solitary cells to keep a few prisoners from being corrupted by evil communication, whilst we hourly expose hundreds of our children to corruption from the same cause; and this

too, at an age, when the mind is much more susceptible of
every impression, whether good or evil? But, tell it not in
New York, neither publish in the streets of Baltimore . . .
If a man should wilfully set fire to his neighbour's house,
he would be severely and deservedly punished. But an un-
lucky boy may, it seems, do it with impunity. At least, he
may "scatter firebrands" as he pleases; and if any mischief
ensues, he escapes, by saying, "Was I not in sport?" Paper
kites are every night set up, with candles to their tails; and
should one of these drop on the roof of a house, Heaven
only knows, what a conflagration might be the conse-
quence. But boys do not regard consequences: and why
should they, if their grey-headed fathers take no pains to
admonish or correct them? It is but a few nights since a
stable was set on fire by a candle from the tail of a kite;
and yet boys are still permitted to go on unmolested, and
hang destruction over our heads; exposing our lives and
property to imminent danger, merely for their amusement! [4]

This editorial gives voice to the sentiments of a concerned
citizen. The indignation seems justified, but in reality, although
the author couldn't have realized it, Philadelphia never had it
so good. Did he feel that Philadelphia should be ashamed to let
New York know what havoc there was in its streets? New York
soon would have no time to worry about Philadelphia. New York
had its own problems, and they were the same problems that
plagued all the major cities in the East, for now, in parts of this
country where there once had seemed to be endless room, there
was crowding and excess.

By the 1790's the supply of slave and wage labor had
reached the point where masters no longer needed apprentices,
and the unattached child was suddenly truly unwanted—not
even his work was in demand. Society still felt some responsi-

[4] Wiley B. Sanders, *Juvenile Offenders for 1000 Years.* Chapel Hill: University of North Carolina Press, 1970, p. 325.

An early nineteenth century woodcut shows Boston boy thieves pursued by city authorities. The hanging figure is a warning to boys with similar intentions.

bility, however, although the sincerity of its concern was questionable; orphanages sprang up pretending to provide the love and care of mothers and fathers, but in reality, they were more like prisons for the young. Nobody in these orphanages was happy, and the bold were quick to escape.

Once out of the orphange, the run-away usually sought out others like himself, and armies of homeless boys wandering about, stealing food, and sleeping in alleyways became a common sight in nineteenth century cities. Little attempt was made to round them up or to return them to the orphanages from which they had escaped. Society had lost both the desire and the ability to police every corner of the community. As long as the armies of boys stayed within certain areas of the city, they had little fear of apprehension and little hope of help.

Outside the cities groups of homeless boys wandered the
roads, stopping in towns to do odd jobs at times but more often
robbing travelers or isolated houses.

Despite these bands of homeless youths, America did not
have a "gang problem" as we know it. Philadelphia might fret
about its delinquent youth and worry about its image in the eyes
of sophisticated New York, but all this would seem trivial in
comparison with things to come.

New York soon felt the first shock waves of a phenomenon
that eventually reached Philadelphia and every other city in the
country, and which spawned an era of gangs that no concerned
citizen in his most pessimistic moments could have forseen.

The phenomenon was immigration. America, "the land of
the free and the home of the brave," was "lifting her lamp" to
light the way for scores of poverty stricken European immigrants "yearning to breathe free." Here was a vast land that
needed to be settled. Unfortunately, most newcomers to America
didn't have enough money to travel any further than the port
cities where they landed, and even those who may have had
enough preferred to stay there anyway, so that they could be
near other immigrants from their native countries.

New York received the greatest influx of immigrants; not
for nothing was the Statue of Liberty erected in the New York
Harbor. Yet although the statue in the harbor symbolized welcome and liberty, the mainland often held in store for these immigrants a degradation the likes of which they had never known
in their homelands. The Irish were the first great wave of immigrants, and it was the Irish who formed the first true New York
City street gangs. Later when the Irish moved to other cities,
gangs would arise there, paralleling the development and activities of the gangs in New York.

The first great wave followed the Revolution and the establishment of the Republic. After all, the Irish hated the British
too, and any conqueror of the British was a friend of theirs. The
majority of the Irish immigrants were poor and settled in New

Although immigrants had high hopes, as the nineteenth century cartoon (top) demonstrates, life in America often meant more hardship than they left behind.

New York Public Library Picture Collection

York where they had landed. In New York, the only neighborhood that would take them was the Five Points district.

Five Points derived its name from the intersection of five
streets, Anthony, Orange, Cross, Little and Mulberry, (today,
Worth, Baxter, Park, and Mulberry streets). The hub of these
five spokes was called Paradise Square, a small park that early
became an entertainment ground for the poor. Children and
blacks peddled mint and strawberries, radishes and hot yams
and Hot Corn Girls sold steaming, roasted ears of corn. Paradise Square was as busy by night as by day. When the children
of the poor, and the day time peddlars retreated to their houses,
the sailors and the gamblers and the pretty Hot Corn Girls came
out. There were fights, certainly, a few robberies, and even a few
killings, but nothing that a single leather-helmeted watchman
could not handle. In fact, Paradise Park and the surrounding
Five Points district remained a comparatively peaceful playground of the poor until about 1820, when the first influx of
Irish immigrants settled there.

After hordes of poor Irish crowded into the Five Points area,
the district began to deteriorate rapidly. Every livable space was
taken over, and by 1837 the Old Brewery, erected in 1792 and
once a producer of world-famous beer, had been transformed
into a honeycomb of squalid living quarters, thieves' hideouts
and fly-by-night prostitution hang-outs. This was not exactly the
new life the Irish had envisioned, but it was the best they
could do.

America was not the land of opportunity the Irish had
heard about. Instead, it was a land of cold and hunger and
squalidness, of discrimination worse than they had known in
their native land. . . . The Irish "increase our taxes, eat our bread
and encumber our streets," wrote Philip Hone, who would later
become Mayor of New York, "and not one in twenty is compe-
tent to keep himself."[5] Although England had traditionally
"solved" its immigration problem by limiting immigration and

---

[5] Allan Nevins, ed., *The Diary of Philip Hone*. New York: Dodd, Mead,
1936, p. 436.

The Five Points in 1829.   *New York Public Library Picture Collection*

thus never letting a problem arise, a comment by an English historian of the time is revealing: "There is a disposition in the United States to use the immigrants, especially the Irish, much as a cat is used in the kitchen to account for broken plates and foods which disappears (sic) . . . New York was not an Eden before the Irish came." [6]

By the early 1820's the Five Points-Paradise Square district was a hell, and pickpockets, murderers, thieves, and all manner of thugs abounded. But until 1825 it was every man for himself; these various criminals did not become organized into working units until one Edward Coleman saw the possibilities of Rosanna Peers' greengrocery.

By the end of the first quarter of the nineteenth century, tiny greengrocery stores had begun to push their way in between the saloons and tenements and houses of prostitution that lined

[6] Edward Robb Ellis, *The Epic of New York City.* New York: Coward-McCann, 1966, p. 232.

the streets of the Five Points district. Ostensibly, their reason for
being was the shortage of produce during those years. Fresh
lettuce and other such vegetables were much too costly for most
of the residents of the area. Partially spoiled or damaged produce, bought for pennies from the ships arriving from the South
or from more high-class markets, was much cheaper, and the
Five Points greengroceries sought to supply the demand. But
for many operators of these greengroceries, the tattered and
brown-streaked produce displayed out front was merely a cover
for shadowy, smoke-filled back rooms, where liquor was sold at
prices considerably cheaper than those at the taverns and saloons. These hidden back rooms attracted the criminal element,
and as the neighborhood candy store would become the hang-out
for the gangs of our era, about 1826 the first organized gang in
New York City was formed in Rosanna Peers' grocery store.

It was the first organized gang because it was the first to
have a definite acknowledged leadership, to adopt a common
name, and to work together for many years. Edward Coleman,
aside from being the leader of the first real gang in New York, is
not particularly important in the annals of gang activity. His
other claim to fame is that he was the first criminal to be
hanged in New York's Tombs Prison. Coleman had fallen in love
with one of the girls who walked the streets each night carrying
a cedar bucket full of roasting ears of corn. She was so attrac-
tive that she was known throughout the area as the Pretty Hot
Corn Girl, and Coleman had married her after fighting at least
a dozen other suitors. After winning his prize, however, Coleman had killed her, because her earnings from the sale of hot
corn failed to meet his expectations. He was put to death in the
Tombs on January 12, 1839.

Coleman, however, had a knack for organization. In 1826,
in the back room of Rosanna Peers' grocery store, he got together
some local thieves and pickpockets and thugs and formed the
Forty Thieves. From this "headquarters" he dispatched the gang
members to rob or murder or beat any well-dressed man or law
enforcement officer foolish enough to enter the district.

New York's second organized gang also had its start in Rosanna Peers' back room. Called the Kerryonians, because its membership traced its roots exclusively to County Kerry, Ireland, this gang was tame compared to the Forty Thieves, and confined itself chiefly to hating the English.

Within a few years other organized gangs like the Forty Thieves were formed in the back rooms of greengroceries: the Chichesters, Roach Guards, Plug Uglies, Shirt Tails, Dead Rabbits. The Chichesters, like the Kerryonians, took their name from the county in Ireland from which they hailed. The Roach Guards originated in the back room of a Five Points liquor store owned by a man named Roach. The Plug Uglies were almost to a man, huge—much larger than the men of the other gangs. Their name came from their large plug hats, which they stuffed with wool and leather to serve as protective helmets in battle. The Shirt Tails distinguished themselves by defying accepted fashion and wearing their shirts outside their trousers. The Dead Rabbits branched off from the Roach Guards. Once during a stormy meeting of the Guards, someone had thrown a dead rabbit into the center of the room, and the dissenting group had seen this as an omen. In Five Points jargon, a rabbit was a tough guy, and a dead rabbit was a super tough guy. When the dissenting faction split from the larger group, they took the name the Dead Rabbits, and their battle standard was a dead rabbit impaled on a pike.

The early gangs turned Paradise Square into a rough and dangerous neighborhood and the area known as the Bowery, not far away, replaced the Five Points district as a recreational center. Theaters, particularly, sprang up in this section, and, to serve their clientele, beer gardens and saloons. But almost as soon as it had been built up as a recreational area, the Bowery began to deteriorate. The beer gardens, especially, became the hang-outs of criminals, and from these headquarters the early Bowery gangs emerged. The largest and most famous was the Bowery Boys, which in time spawned dozens of off-shoots. Other Bowery gangs of note were the True Blue Americans, the

The Bowery Boys as depicted in a contemporary lithograph.
New York Public Library Picture Collection

American Guards, the O'Connell Guards, and the Atlantic Guards. In general, although they engaged in numerous street brawls and certain types of thievery, they were not as criminal or as violent as the Paradise Square gangs. Perhaps this was because the Bowery was still a more respectable, less squalid neighborhood than the Five Points district.

The chief activity of the Bowery gangs was street brawling with the Paradise Square gangs. They fought over territory just as gangs fight over "turf" in the twentieth century. In Paradise Square, although the Roach Guards and Dead Rabbits constantly fought each other, they forgot their differences when facing the Bowery gangs and fought side by side.

The most bitter and longest-lasting feud was between the Dead Rabbits and the Bowery Boys. From the 1830's to the 1860's hardly a week passed that the Dead Rabbits, supported by the other Five Points gangs, and the Bowery Boys, flanked by the other Bowery gangs, did not engage in battle. Sometimes

A battle between the Bowery Boys and the Dead Rabbits.
New York Public Library Picture Collection

these battles lasted two or three days, endless melees of beating, maiming and murder.

On the outskirts of the battle were the women, ready to supply ammunition, to give medical aid, to watch for a break in the enemy's defense, sometimes even to jump into the fray. The most notable female fighter was Hell-Cat Maggie, who fought alongside the leaders of the Dead Rabbits during the 1840's. Legend has it that her teeth were filed to sharp points and that she wore long, artificial fingernails made of brass.

The police were sometimes able to quell the fray—at considerable physical risk. Any officer caught by either gang faced beating, torture, maiming or even death. Often they were forced to ask the assistance of the National Guard and the regular Army. Regiments of soldiers in full battle dress marching through the streets to the scene of a gang melee, were not an uncommon sight in New York. Generally, they had no trouble dispersing the gangs.

Nineteenth century toughs "hang out" on a street corner.
New York Public Library Picture Collection

What were they like, these early gangs and their members? How do they compare with the gangs of today? For the most part they were Irish, joining together in the face of poverty, squalid conditions, and great prejudice. In general, they were older than the gang members of today, although a considerable number were in their late teens. The products of unhealthy slums and malnutrition, they averaged, with the exception of the taller Plug Uglies, only about 5'3" in height and weighed between 120 and 135 pounds. Their gangs were considerably larger than those of today, numbering in the hundreds; one gang claimed 1,200 members.

In addition to their distinctive names, they sported distinctive dress. All of the Five Points gangs usually fought in their undershirts. The Roach Guards wore a blue stripe on their pantaloons, the Dead Rabbits a red stripe. Of all the Bowery gangs, the True Blue Americans wore the most distinctive uniforms, stove pipe hats and ankle length frock coats.

The weapons the gangs used were deadly and imaginative. Some were fortunate enough to own pistols and muskets, but the usual weapons were knives and brickbats and bludgeons. For close work there were brass knuckles, ice picks, pikes and other interesting paraphernalia.

These gang members enjoyed their "work" and evidently violence "just for kicks" is not a twentieth century phenomenon. Gangs of the early nineteenth century engaged in it frequently:

> One strolled up to an old man sipping beer and hacked open his scalp with a huge bludgeon. Asked why, the ruffian replied, "Well, I had forty-nine nicks in my stick, an' I wanted to make it an even fifty." Another Plug Ugly seized a stranger and cracked his spine in three places just to win a two-dollar bet.[7]

It did not take unscrupulous and shrewd politicians long to realize the gangs and their talents could be utilized in a num-

[7] Ibid., p. 233.

ber of ways, as long as they were kept under control. In the early 1830's many ward and district leaders acquired title to the grocery stores in Five Points and the saloons and dance halls in the Bowery where the gangs hung out. They assured protection to the gangs' meeting places, and offered financial rewards to the gangs for their loyalty. Gang leaders were paid for taking care of jobs like blackjacking political opponents and voting many times over at the polls. Nearly every shrewd ward and district leader had at least one gang working for him. Thus the gangs of New York played no small part in the political struggles of the mid-nineteenth century, starting under the approving eye of the politicians, a great series of riots as well as hundreds of battles and fights. In so doing, however, the gangs had in part neutralized their ferocious images. After all, they had, in essence, joined the *establishment;* however fearsome they might be, they were controllable.

The river front gangs who had meanwhile sprung up along the docks and shipyards owed allegiance to no one but themselves. They took up where the Five Points and Bowery gangs had left off. The waterfront gangs were more violent—while the Five Points and Bowery gangs were primarily thieves and street brawlers, and only occasionally murderers, the dock gangs were out-and-out killers and robbers. They seldom engaged in street brawls, but when they did they usually emerged victorious. Even the Dead Rabbits and the Plug Uglies were no match for their ferociousness. The river boys also tended to be younger. The first real river front gang was the Daybreak Boys, so-named because they usually conducted their activities at dawn. Herbert Asbury wrote of its members:

> Nicholas Saul and William Howlett, who were hanged in the Tombs when the former was but twenty years old and Howlett a year his junior, were the most celebrated leaders of the Daybreak Boys, although the membership of the gang included many noted criminals, among them Slobbery Jim, Sow Madden, Gow-legged Sam McCarthy and

A nineteenth century illustration satirizes the city's up and coming generation.   *New York Public Library Picture Collection*

Patsy the Barber. None of these thugs was more than twenty years old when he had acquired a reputation as a murderous gangster and cutthroat, and there was scarcely a man among them who had not committed at least one murder, and innumerable robberies, before he reached his majority. Saul and Howlett joined the gang when they were sixteen and fifteen, respectively, and several others were even younger; a few were as young as ten and twelve years old.[8]

Other waterfront gangs included the Short Tails, the Border Gang, and the Swamp Angels. All of these gangs operated on the East River side of Manhattan, pirating the cargo on the ships and docks, murdering watchmen and unsuspecting passers-by. Often, their pirating activities involved rowing out

[8] Herbert Asbury, *The Gangs of New York: An Informal History of the Underworld.* New York: Alfred A. Knopf, 1927, pp. 66–67.

to ships anchored in the river. That is one reason why they confined themselves to the East River; the waters of the Hudson were considerably more treacherous. Then, too, most of the Hudson River piers were used by ocean-going vessels, whose owners saw to it that their docks were well-lighted and adequately guarded. The one gang of note to work the Hudson River docks was the Charleston Street Gang. Because the docks were so difficult to plunder, they eventually stole a small sloop and sailed up and down the Hudson, robbing farmhouses and riverside towns and kidnapping children to hold for ransom.

The river gangs, who were not protected by any of the city's political factions, were more seriously fought by the authorities than the inland gangs. In 1858 the city leaders agreed to the organization of a harbor police. In the spring of that year over a dozen row boats manned by experienced policemen began to patrol the dock areas, investigating every suspicious looking vessel. Their chief target was the Daybreak Boys, and the gang was practically destroyed by the end of 1859. Other river gangs, however, continued to exist until the end of the Civil War, enjoying a particularly profitable period in 1863, when the attentions of the police were directed elsewhere.

The decade before the Civil War was a heyday for most of New York's street gangs. In New York, there was all-out corruption of the city government under the Tammany Hall political organization. Graft was so widespread that most of the police force did nothing but collect payoffs and do favors for the politicians. The few honest policemen were practically powerless to control the gangs, for everytime they made an arrest some indignant politician arrived demanding the criminals' release.

Gang membership swelled considerably during this decade, as criminals from other cities hurried to New York looking for a piece of the corruption pie. By 1855 it was estimated that there were at least 30,000 who owed allegiance to the gang leaders and, through them, to politicians of various factions. At every election the gangs burned ballot boxes, beat up ordinary citizens

Upsetting the voting booth—one of the ways gangs influenced the election returns.   *New York Public Library Picture Collection*

trying to exercise their right to vote, and themselves voted many times over. When policemen tried to guard the polls, they were soundly beaten.

By 1857 the police force was so corrupt that the New York State legislature stepped in. It got rid of the Municipal Police and set up a new Metropolitan Police force under the control of a special board appointed by the Governor. Mayor Fernando Wood, however, refused to recognize these orders, and there ensued a fierce struggle between the Metropolitans and the Municipals for City Hall. Not until the Seventh Regiment of the National Guard stepped in did the Metropolitans emerge victorious.

The gangsters and other criminals took advantage of the chaotic situation, plundering stores and businesses and private

The Five Points in 1859.   *New York Public Library Picture Collection*

homes without fear of police interference. The gangs of the Five Points district and the Bowery embarked upon a period of street brawling that has been described as "the most ferocious free-for-all in the history of the city." [9] Not until several National Guard units were called was the rioting quelled. In the accounts of the riots, the police and newspapers, among them *The New York Times*, described the gangs as being composed of thieves and criminals, and this disturbed one of the Five Points gangs, the Dead Rabbits. They were very concerned with their image:

> "We are requested by the Dead Rabbits," said the *Times*, "to state that the Dead Rabbit club members are not thieves, that they did not participate in the riot with the

[9] Ibid., p. 113.

Bowery Boys, and that the fight in Mulberry Street was between the Roach Guards of Mulberry Street and the Atlantic Guards of the Bowery. The Dead Rabbits are sensitive on points of honor, we are assured, and wouldn't allow a thief to live on their beat, much less to be a member of their club." [10]

After the Police Riots, the city remained fairly calm until 1863, when rioting occurred that seemed destined to destroy the city.

In March, 1863, Congress passed the Conscription Act which gave the President power to draft citizens into military service. In April, President Lincoln issued a proclamation calling for 300,000 men, and in May the War Department announced that the draft would begin in New York City on July 11th. Across the country there was widespread opposition to the Conscription Act, chiefly because it contained a clause that exempted any drafted man who paid the government $300. Naturally, this meant that the poor would form the bulk of those drafted, and between March and July there was much speechmaking and editorialized criticism of this clause.

July 11th was approaching but New York City authorities did not feel the need to prepare in any special way for the people's reaction to the draft. On July 11th they appeared to have been right, although ominous mutterings could be heard among the men who gathered on street corners the day the majority of the names were drawn for the draft.

By Sunday, July 12th, however, there was an unusual flurry of activity among the gangs. The leaders sent messages back and forth, many containing reports that rich men whose names had been drawn had already paid their three hundred dollars to get out of the draft. At 6:00 A.M. on Monday, small crowds of men and women began to emerge from the tenements and flophouses of the West Side and to move northward along Eighth and Ninth Avenues. They were joined along the way by other

[10] Ibid., p. 117.

small crowds and by individual workers, who left their jobs.
Meanwhile, a similar group was making its way up the East
Side, and in a vacant lot east of Central Park, the two gangs
met and became a throng. Shouting defiance of the government
the mob made its way to the draft office at Third Avenue and
Forty-Sixth Street, where the drawing of names for the draft
continued.

Although estimates of the crowd varied, one observer noted
that it took about twenty-five minutes for the crowd to pass a
given point and that they filled Forty-Seventh Street from curb
to curb. Police rushed to form a barricade around the draft office,
and then someone in the crowd raised a pistol and fired. For the
next six days New York raged with more rioting and fighting
than it had ever known and would ever know again. The Provost
Marshal's Office on Third Avenue was burned as well as the
Second Avenue Armory; Police Stations, bridges, and fine private residences were looted and burned. Countless businesses
were ransacked, and scores of police and innocent citizens were
beaten and killed.

At first, several of the city's newspapers had been sympathetic to the mob, referring to the rioters as *the people* and
their anger against the Conscription Act as just, but soon they
were forced to agree with *The New York Times:*

> This mob is not the people, nor does it belong to the
> people. It is for the most part made up of the vilest ele-
> ments in the city. It has not even the poor merit of being
> what mobs usually are—the product of mere ignorance and
> passion. They talk, or rather they did talk at first, of the
> oppressiveness of the Conscription Law; but three-fourths
> of those who have been actively engaged in violence have
> been boys and young men twenty years of age, and not at
> all subject to the Conscription. Were the Conscription Law
> to be abrogated tomorrow, the controlling inspiration would
> remain the same.[11]

[11] Ibid., p. 118.

The controlling inspiration of the mob was to destroy the city, and secondly to destroy the city's Negro population.

The census of 1860 had shown that of the 813,669 people living in New York City, a little more than half were foreign-born. Of the foreign-born residents, the Irish, with 203,740, were the largest group and they also constituted the overwhelming majority of poor people. They were at the lower rung of the economic and social ladder and had no love for blacks, who were competing for the same low-paying jobs.

During the decade before the Civil War, the animosity toward blacks was heightened, and in the wild abandon of the draft riots the mob finally vented its pent-up hatred. Three black men were hanged on the first day of the rioting, and each day afterward an average of three others were found hanged, their bodies burned or maimed by the women who followed in the

A black man, lynched and burned during the Draft Riots.
New York Public Library Picture Collection

An angry mob burns the Colored Orphan Asylum during the Draft Riots.
Museum of the City of New York

wake of the male rioters. On the first day, the crowd also burned the Colored Orphan Asylum on Fifth Avenue between Forty-third and Forty-fourth Streets, killing a little girl who had been overlooked by employees and police in the rush to evacuate the Asylum. Rioting occurred in every Negro section of the city.

On Tuesday evening the Governor of New York declared the city in a state of siege and by early Wednesday evening several thousand troops, soldiers in the war against the Confederacy, had arrived to reinforce the helpless police. Thursday was the last day of serious fighting, and only a few incidents occurred Friday and Saturday. The Draft Riots were over, leaving in their wake incredible tolls in life and property. At least 2000 people were killed and another 8000 wounded. Most of the casualties were rioters. Only three policemen died, although nearly every man in the force was wounded. The military units suffered 50 deaths. More than one hundred buildings were burned and the property loss amounted to five million dollars. Thousands of New Yorkers who had fled the city did not return for months. The city was exhausted and spent, and yet the violence had not come to an end. Gangsters and criminals continued to set fires and loot businesses all during the remaining years of the Civil War.

In the twenty years following the Civil War, New York society was characterized by corruption and vice. Almost every criminal of note in the United States made New York his headquarters, and during this era "the fence" business, receiving and selling stolen property, thrived. Robbery, murder, and beatings were so flagrant that many of the old-time street brawling gangs faded in importance. The Chichesters, in fact, disbanded. But other, more ferocious gangs, arose to commit the crimes and do the dirty work that the old gangs hadn't the stomach for.

The greatest of the post Civil War gangs, the Whyos, was actually formed by some of the former Chichesters. The name of the gang seems to have come from a weird cry they sometimes uttered. Their headquarters was in Mulberry Bend, near the

The Whyo gang's headquarters.
The Jacob A. Riis Collection, Museum of the City of New York

Five Points, and from there they ranged throughout the city.
Although they engaged in fights with other gangs, and also
were expert thieves, their chief concern was murder. During
this period they were supposed not to accept a new member
until he had committed at least one murder. Beating, maiming
and killing were activities so respected by the gang that certain
members were known to advertise their services and price lists.
One, Piker Ryan, carried the following list:

Punching	$ 2
Both eyes blackened	$ 4
Nose and jaw broke	$ 10
Jacked out (knocked out with a blackjack)	$ 15
Ear chewed off	$ 15
Leg or arm broke	$ 19
Shot in leg	$ 25
Stab	$ 25
Doing the big job	$100 and up [12]

Another prominent band, the Gophers, ruled over Hell's
Kitchen, a rough West Side neighborhood. Their name was derived from their fondness for hiding in basements or cellars.
There was so much jealousy among the Gophers, that no leader
held his post for more than a few months. Certain names stood
out among them though, such as One Lung Curran, who may be
the first gang member in history to start the fashion of distinctive jackets. The story goes that One Lung's girl complained
that he did not have a suitable fall coat, whereupon he went out
into the street, blackjacked the first policeman he met, and re-
moved the officer's uniform blouse. One Lung's girl stitched the
blouse into a smart jacket of military style. It was so admired
by the other Gophers that they all promptly blackjacked policemen and stole their blouses. For some time a policeman could
not pass through the Gopher's area and remain fully clothed.

[12] Ibid., p. 228.

The Gophers, the Eastmans, the Five Pointers, Gas Housers, and Hudson Dusters were the principal gangs of the period. In addition, there were many independent gangs that controlled small areas within the territories of the larger gangs and fiercely maintained their independence. Small areas of the Hudson Duster domain were controlled by the Marginals, the Pearl Buttons and the Fashion Plates, while the Eastman kingdom contained the smaller kingdoms of the Fourteenth Street Gang, the Yakey Yakes, the Lollie Meyers and the Red Onions.

The post Civil War period saw the rise of gangs of nationalities other than Irish, and not just in northern cities. It was at this time that the Ku Klux Klan arose in the South. When it began, the Klan was not unlike other youthful gangs. Most, if not all, of the six young men who started the Klan were veterans of the Civil War and had returned home to find their town, Pulaski, Tennessee, and the rest of the South in a state of extreme economic and social disorganization. There was neither money nor jogs for returning soldiers and not very much to do. Discouraged and bored, the six young men decided to form some sort of club, some group with an air of mystery and exclusiveness that might make life more exciting.

Like other gangs, the group considered name and dress very important. One of the young men had gone to college for awhile and had suggested the use of the Greek word *kuklos*, which means band or circle. They decided to split the word and to substitute a "ux" for "os" in the second half, resulting in Ku Klux. Since all six members were of Scottish descent, it was decided to add the word *clan* to the name, changing the "c" to a "k" for consistency.

Their goals, at first, were extremely simple. They stood for purity and for preservation of the home and for protection of the orphans of Confederate soldiers. Their "colors" symbolized these goals—white for purity and red for the blood they were ready to shed in defense of the helpless. Not just by coincidence, red and white had also been the colors of the Confederacy. For

Two Klansmen.

To Change the World: A Picture Story of Reconstruction, by Milton Meltzer

costumes, they used sheets and pillow cases and dressed up themselves and their horses. Then, they rode slowly and silently through the streets of Pulaski. White passers-by were amused at the procession, but according to legend, blacks who happened to witness the parade were not. Word spread that the costumes of the Ku Klux Klan had frightened the blacks, and other whites eagerly sought to join. The trouble was, these others were interested in frightening and hurting blacks, not really in upholding the goals set by the founders.

Southern whites at this time, at least in their own eyes, were in a situation similar to that of the immigrant and minority groups in the North who formed gangs. Under the Reconstruction Acts passed by Congress in 1867, the South was occupied by federal troops. The majority of Southerners had supported the Confederacy and so were denied the right to vote or to hold public office. They were forced to watch hopelessly as newly-enfranchised blacks and northern intruders won major public offices.

As a result, white Southerners saw themselves as a downtrodden minority, discriminated against, denied any status or identity. To many, the Klan, with its secrecy and its costumes that made excellent disguises, was the perfect means of revenge. Within a year there were hundreds of groups in towns throughout the South calling themselves the Ku Klux Klan, with costumes and stated goals similar to those of the Pulaski Klan. Where they differed was in their activities, which ranged from pranks to frighten blacks to severe physical punishment of blacks and white northern "carpetbaggers." As each Klan was independent of the others, there was no central authority to curb the excesses.

All across the South the Klansmen roamed, and at their peak they numbered one million, lynching "uppity niggers," whipping northern school teachers for treating blacks as equals, threatening and intimidating anyone who dared question the idea of white supremacy.

Then, in 1877, the government changed its southern policy. The Reconstruction Acts were repealed and federal troops were withdrawn from the South. Suddenly, Southerners were in power again and in a short time they had taken away most of the rights that had been given the blacks under Reconstruction. Although blacks weren't legally re-enslaved, they were reduced again to virtual slavery. For southern whites, things were back to normal.

The Ku Klux Klan became inactive. With the Northerners gone and the blacks "back in their place," the Klan had nothing to do. Although there have been attempts to revive it since, the Klan has never regained its former size and power.

The Short Tail gang poses in their dockside hideout.
The Jacob A. Riis Collection, Museum of the City of New York

While the Klan was terrorizing the South, German gangs were forming in the North. In New York, about 1868, the Hell's Kitchen Gang came into being under the leadership of Dutch Heinrichs. For several years the gang terrorized the Hell's Kitchen district, robbing and beating strangers, breaking into houses and businesses, and demanding pay-offs from the merchants in the area. A few years later the first Mafiosi began operations and set up their own standards of law and order along Mulberry Street where the first Italian community arose.

By the post Civil War period, more than half a century had passed since the appearance of the first organized gang. There were now thousands of gangs and satellites of gangs, and their activities were considerably more sophisticated. The practice of using knockout drops on victims became popular—the drug enabled the thieves or murderers to drag the body into an alley or basement and go about their business at leisure. There were gangs who specialized in grave robbing; one gang, the Hartley Mob, always traveled in a hearse, finding it easy to pass by police and other gangs who respectfully made way for the funeral procession.

Yet the gangs of the 70's, 80's and 90's were not very different from those of the 20's, 30's and 40's. They had colorful names—the Molasses Gang, the Battle Row Gang, the Dutch Mob, the Rag Gang, the Gas House Gang, the Stable Gang, the Potaskes, the Silver Gang—which were taken from their neighborhoods, from their modes of operation and from numerous other sources. They dressed to be noticed and often hats identified the gang; one gang sported derbies, another, slouch hats, another, no hats at all. While the earlier gangs met in back rooms of greengroceries, or the halls of saloons, these gangs had their "clubrooms" usually in tenements, where they slept, drank, played cards and planned their raids. Like their predecessors they came from the slums, which now dotted the city, from the tenements and cramped living quarters of the poor, and like their predecessors they joined together for identity, for a sense of adventure, for a sense of *being somebody*. Jacob Riis, whose photographs and writings of "the other half" of society are still the greatest documents of lower class life of the time, wrote of the gangs:

> . . . it might be inferred that the New York tough is a very fierce individual, of indomitable courage and naturally as blood-thirsty as a tiger. On the contrary he is an errant coward. His instincts of ferocity are those of the wolf rather than the tiger. It is only when he hunts with the pack that he is dangerous. Then his inordinate vanity makes him forget all fear or caution in the desire to distinguish himself before his fellows, a result of his swallowing all the flash literature and penny-dreadfuls he can beg, borrow, or steal —and there is never any lack of them—and of the strongly dramatic element in his nature that is nursed by such a diet into rank and morbid growth . . . an intense love of show and applause . . . I have a very vivid recollection of seeing one of his tribe, a robber and murderer before he was nineteen, go to the gallows unmoved, all fear of the rope overcome, as it seemed, by the secret exultant pride of being the centre of a first-class show, shortly to be followed by that acme of tenement-life bliss, the big funeral.[13]

Like its predecessors, the gang of the post Civil War period was also very interested in publicity, and it was given a great deal. "The newspapers chronicle its doings daily," Riis wrote disapprovingly, "with a sensational minuteness of detail that does its share toward keeping up its evil traditions and inflaming the ambition of its members to be as bad as the worst." [14] Riis always found willing subjects when he wanted to photograph the gangs. In fact, the toughs crowded into the picture, striking comic poses. One gang, the Montgomery Guards, even demon-

[13] Jacob Riis, *How the Other Half Lives*. New York: Dover Publishers, 1971, pp. 173–174.
[14] Ibid., p. 171.

A group portrait of the Montgomery Guards.
The Jacob A. Riis Collection, Museum of the City of New York

strated their mugging technique for the camera. A gang who caught the fancy of the newspaper reporters was guaranteed more power just by the magical quality of having its name in print, and because of newspapers the names of these gangs lived on, long after the gangs themselves dissolved: the Gophers, the Whyos, the Hudson Dusters. Often gang members boasted of committing brutal crimes just for kicks. Riis recalled the arrest of two of the Montgomery Guards who robbed a Jewish peddlar and then bragged of trying to saw off his head . . ."just for fun." [15]

Yet, with all this, the gangs of the 70's, 80's and 90's were just as concerned about their "image" as the Dead Rabbits who had asked *The New York Times* to make it clear that they were not a gang at all, but a "social club."

"He does not steal;" wrote Riis, "he 'wins' your money or your watch . . . he passes around the hat for 'voluntary' contributions . . ." [16]

> Drunk and foul mouthed, ready to cut the throat of a defenseless stranger at the toss of a cent, fresh from beating his decent mother black and blue to get money for rum, he will resent as an intolerable insult the imputation that he is 'no gentleman.' Fighting the battles with the coward's weapons, the brass-knuckles and the deadly sand-bag, or with brick-bats from the housetops, he is still in all seriousness a lover of fair play and as likely as not, when his gang has downed a policeman in a battle that has cost a dozen broken heads, to be found next saving a drowning child or woman at the peril of his own life.[17]

Unlike their predecessors, the gangs of the post Civil War period were quite frequently drug users. Countless soldiers had returned from the war addicted to the morphine they had been given to ease the pain of their wounds. The drug was available in

[15] Ibid., p. 174.
[16] Ibid., p. 180.
[17] Ibid., p. 172.

most stores. Laudanum, another depressant, was also available, but until the practice of using knockout drops on their victims became popular among the gangs, laudanum was chiefly a "female" drug (women sometimes "swooned" in those days not because they were more fragile than women today but because they were addicted to laudanum.) Once the gangs bought it in quantity they naturally tried it themselves. But by far the most popular drug among the gangs was the stimulant cocaine.

"Perhaps ninety percent of the [Hudson] Dusters were cocaine addicts," wrote Herbert Asbury, "and when under the influence of the drug were very dangerous, for they were insensible to ordinary punishment, and were possessed of great, if artificial bravery and ferocity." [18]

And unlike society in the 1820's, 30's and 40's with its Philip Hones and its other outraged citizenry, society in the 1870's, 80's and 90's at least tried to understand the gangs.

The post war period was a time of tremendous growth in the United States. New industries were springing up, workers were needed to man these new industries, and so immigration was encouraged. Within the space of a few years thousands of immigrants arrived, settling in the cities where industry was concentrated and where they could find others of their kind. Landlords quickly divided up their apartment buildings to accommodate and cheat the newcomers. "Respectable citizens" hastened to erect invisible but all too real barriers to keep the newcomers out. But as wave upon wave of immigrants flowed into the cities, it became impossible to make those barriers high enough. The poverty, the hunger, the misery of the immigrants was a reality too stark to be shut out. The "respectable citizenry" realized that perhaps there was more involved in the problem than they had originally thought.

Perhaps the poor were poor not because of laziness or choice but because of the conditions in which they were forced to live,

[18] Asbury, p. 238.

An Italian immigrant cradling her child against the squalor of tenement life.   *The Jacob A. Riis Collection, Museum of the City of New York*

because of the tenements where there was not even room to breathe, because of the squalor, because of the oppression, because of the utter hopelessness that there could ever be any way out.

The first true reform movement in history arose. In the forefront of this movement was Jacob Riis, a Danish immigrant himself. Riis was concerned about all the facets and results of poverty and oppression, including the gangs. In writing about gangs, he often referred to "the growler," which was a mug for liquor or beer:

The 'growler' stood at the cradle of the tough. It bosses him through his boyhood apprenticeship in the 'gang', and leaves him to finish his training and turns him loose upon the world to thief, to collect by stealth or by force the living his philosophy tells him that it owes him, and will not voluntarily surrender without an equivalent in the work which he hates. From the moment he, almost a baby, for the first time carries the growler for beer, he is never out of its reach, and the two soon form a partnership that lasts through life. It has at least the merit, such as it is, of being loyal. The saloon is the only thing that takes kindly to the lad. Honest play is interdicted in the streets. The policeman arrests the ball-tossers, and there is no room in the back-yard. In one of these, between two enormous tenements that swarmed with children, I read this ominous notice:

'All boys caught in this yard will be dealt with according to law.' [19]

The purpose of the reform movement was to improve the life of the poor, and that meant changing conditions that gave rise to the gangs. Ironically, however, the reform movement helped the growth of the gang population through the passage of the Child Labor laws.

Reformers had been shocked in 1873 to find that some 100,000 children worked in the factories in New York for long hours and little pay. A massive campaign was mounted against child labor, and the minimum age at which a child could work was moved up to 10, then to 12, and eventually to 16. Such laws were needed, to be sure, but an unexpected problem arose. One hundred thousand former child laborers were now idle. There was a hasty movement to build asylums, camps, orphanages, missions and schools, but the street claimed a large number. There were more than 10,000 of those "street Arabs" as Jacob Riis called them, in New York in the 1870's. While there were some juvenile gangs before the Civil War, now their number increased enormously.

[19] Riis, p. 171.

A child factory worker beside the machine he mans.
Lewis Hine Collection, the Library of Congress

Two "street Arabs" who make their homes in doorways and back alleys.
The Jacob A. Riis Collection, Museum of the City of New York

Although they had their own officers and organizations,
these juvenile gangs were generally under the control of the
adult gangs.

"There were the Forty Little Thieves, the Little Dead Rabbits, and the Little Plug Uglies," wrote Herbert Asbury, "the
members of which emulated their elders in speech and
deed, and as far as possible in appearance. And in the
Fourth Ward, along the water front, were the Little Daybreak Boys, composed of lads from eight to twelve years of
age, who were almost as ferocious as the older gangsters
whose name they adopted and whose crimes they strove
mightily to imitate. Some accompanied the Daybreak Boys
on various enterprises, acting as lookouts and decoys, and
crawling through the portholes of ships and lowering ropes
up which the adult thugs clambered to the decks. But they
also planned and executed many adventures of their own
account, and were believed by the police to have committed
several murders." [20]

For a while the Forty Little Thieves were led by a girl, Wild
Maggie Carson, until, at 12, she was persuaded to go straight by
a concerned minister.

Juvenile gangs poured forth from all the poverty and slum
pockets of the city, from neighborhoods with such descriptive
names as Rotten Row, Poverty Lane, and Misery Row. The
Nineteenth Street Gang and the Fourth Avenue Tunnel Gang
were particularly notorious. Like their elders, they engaged in
gang fights, maintained club houses, admired bravado and usually committed crimes only in groups.

"Of the 82,200 persons arrested by the police in 1889,"
wrote Jacob Riis, "10,505 were under twenty years old. The
last report of the Society for the Prevention of Cruelty to
Children enumerates as 'a few typical cases,' eighteen 'pro-
fessional cracksmen' between nine and fifteen years old,

[20] Asbury, p. 239.

who had been caught with burglar's tools, or in the act of robbery. Four of them, hardly yet in long trousers, had 'held up' a wayfarer in the public street and robbed him of $75. One, aged sixteen, was the leader of a noted gang of young robbers in Forty-Ninth Street. He committed murder, for which he is now serving a term of nineteen years in State's Prison. Four of the eighteen were girls and quite as bad as the worst." [21]

The dawning of the twentieth century brought with it the beginning of widespread use of firearms by the gangs, especially in their wars among themselves. While the old-time gangsters had used brickbats, brass knuckles, clubs, teeth and fists, and only occasionally a pistol, now almost every gangster carried at least two pistols, and some carried as many as four. The gang members liked to show off their weapons but in 1911 the Sullivan Law made possession of a firearm a prison offense. Thereafter guns were concealed in pockets and hats and strapped to legs under trousers.

In 1903 the use of guns in a war between the Eastmans and the Five Pointers provoked such terror that the general public, used to hearing of a murder here and there, finally realized just how much power the gangs had, and the politicians, who were still providing legal protection for the gangs, were forced to take their dangerous henchmen to task. Although the gangs had been feuding for two years, it was not until August of 1903 that the war reached a climax. The Eastmans and the Five Pointers massed on either side of the elevated railroad structure on Rivington Street and opened fire. Innocent passers-by rushed for cover; storekeepers barricaded their doors and windows; frightened citizens huddled behind locked doors. A detachment of Gophers happened upon the scene and, delighted to find some action, plunged into the fighting, firing at Five Pointers and Eastmans alike. Hours later, police reserves charged down Rivington Street with their pistols blazing and the gangsters scattered. In their

[21] Riis, p. 178.

wake the gangs left three dead, seven seriously wounded, and some 20 captured by the police.

The next morning every newspaper carried reports of the brawl and indignant editorials demanded an end to such terror. The politicians realized the gangs had gone too far, and although they provided bail for the imprisoned, hospital care for the wounded and burial for the dead, as was their usual custom, this time the politicians also arranged a meeting between the leader of the Eastmans, Monk Eastman, and the leader of the Five Pointers, Paul Kelly, and made it clear that if a truce did not result from the meeting, neither gang would be in business any longer. In the face of such persuasion, Eastman and Kelly did indeed declare a truce, the first truce between gangs to be established at the urging of outside forces. But while gang activity was being subdued in the Bowery and Five Points districts, it was flaring up elsewhere, this time in Chinatown.

Before the influx of Chinese, the area that became Chinatown was inhabited chiefly by Germans, and a few Irish. In 1858 a Cantonese named Ah Ken came to New York, settled in Mott Street and opened a cigar store. Ten years later, a man named Wah Kee arrived and established a combination grocery-curio business on Pell Street, which intersects Mott. In 1872 there was a total of just 12 Chinese people in the district. Then the United States, which was industrializing rapidly and needed cheap labor for all its new railroads and factories, began actively to recruit Orientals, and the flood was on. In 1880 there were 700 Chinese living in the area, and by 1910 there were between 10,000 and 15,000. As their number grew, the Chinese formed secret associations, or *tongs*, which first were just mutual aid societies whose membership depended on which province in China a person was from. Eventually, however, the tongs became powerful and often violent groups which ran gambling houses, opium dens, and white slave rings.

Wah Kee, the second recorded Chinese to arrive in the Mott and Pell Street area, was the first to engage in illegal activities.

THE CHINESE QUARTER IN MOTT ST — A FRESH ARRIVAL FROM CALIFORNIA

An illustrated weekly depicts newly arrived immigrants to New York's Chinatown at the turn of the century.

Museum of the City of New York

He used his grocery-curio store as a front for gambling games and opium-smoking quarters on the floor above. He did an excellent business, attracting the lower class thugs from neighboring districts, and before long other arriving Chinese who came to New York were following his lead. By the middle of the 1890's there were some 200 gambling houses in Chinatown, and almost as many opium dens. Most of these were controlled by a single tong, the On Leongs, led by one Tom Lee and protected by fierce henchmen dressed in shirts of chain mail. The other tong involved in gambling was the Hip Sings, led by Wong Get, and they operated their games only at the consent of the On Leongs. Police and politicians were very tolerant of these illegal activities, and with only one tong having any real power, all was peaceful in Chinatown throughout the 1890's.

Early in 1900, however, a man named Mock Duck arrived in Chinatown. Although he did not belong to any tongs there, he sported the garb of the tong killers—a shirt of chain mail—and carried two guns in addition to a hatchet. Upon his arrival, he announced his intention to rule Chinatown himself and promptly set about upsetting the On Leong operations in every way possible. The Hip Sings welcomed the arrival of Mock Duck and formed an alliance with him, and within a year Mock Duck was leader of the Hip Sings and had greatly increased its membership. Now it was time to mount a concerted attack on the On Leongs.

A few weeks later a mysterious fire destroyed an On Leong boarding house on Pell Street, killing two On Leong members. Tom Lee immediately sent one of his henchmen out to kill the first Hip Sing member he saw for revenge. Then the fight was on. A small tong, the Four Brothers, joined the Hip Sings and together they made every effort to kill Tom Lee. When they failed, Mock Duck decided to try a different method to destroy his rival; he went to the authorities and gave the address of every big On Leong gambling house. In short order, these houses were raided and closed down by the police, and then quickly reopened under Hip Sing control. Naturally, the On Leongs were determined to regain their lost businesses, and the war continued until 1906, when the public became so alarmed at the violence that the authorities arranged a peace treaty between the tongs. The On Leongs were given control of all vice in Mott Street and the Hip Sings supremacy in Pell Street.

Except for a few minor disturbances, the treaty remained in effect for three years. Ironically, the incident that caused the break in 1909 began in San Francisco. There, a slave girl who had been sold by her father in Canton and brought to the United States, was purchased for $3000 by Low Hee Tong, a member of the San Francisco branch of the Four Brothers. The girl, Bow Kum, lived with Low Hee Tong until he was arrested and the police found that Bow Kum was not his legal bride. She was then taken from him and sent to a Christian Mission. She left the mission when she married a truck gardener named Tchin Len, who brought her to New York.

Low Hee Tong apparently didn't mind the loss of the girl. He did, however, mind the loss of his $3000, and he demanded that Tchin Len pay him this sum. Tchin Len refused. Low Hee Tong refused to give up. He wrote a letter to the Four Brothers and Hip Sings in New York, asking their help. Always eager to help a brother in the West, the Four Brothers and Hip Sings presented Low Hee Tong's demand to the On Leongs, of which Tchin Len was a member. The On Leongs ignored the demand, and the Four Brothers and the Hip Sings declared war.

On August 15, 1909, a Four Brothers-Hip Sings killer broke into Tchin Len's house and slashed the girl, Bow Kum, to death. Killing after killing followed.

By 1910, when a treaty was finally worked out, with the aid of the Chinese Minister in Washington, some fifty people had been killed and many more injured. Great, too, was the loss and damage of property, for the Chinese had begun to experiment with dynamite, and many bombings were recorded.

Chinatown was relatively peaceful until 1912, when a new tong, the Kim Lan Wui Saw, arose and boldly declared war on both the On Leongs and the Hip Sings. The two older gangs united to destroy the intruders and were enjoying success until the authorities again stepped in and forced all factions to sign yet another treaty. Peace reigned once again in Chinatown and would do so for the next 12 years.

Meanwhile, in the rest of the city, the gangs had by no means been inactive, and outbursts of violence, first on the East Side, then on the West Side, continued. Jacob Riis wrote:

It is a peculiarity of the gangs that they usually break out in spots, as it were. When the West Side is in a state of

A portrait of the reformer Jacob Riis.   *Museum of the City of New York*

eruption, the East Side gangs "lie low," and when the toughs along the North River are nursing broken heads at home, or their revenge in Sing Sing, fresh trouble breaks out in the tenements east of Third Avenue. This result is brought about by the very efforts made by the police to put down the gangs . . . The gangs belt the city like a huge chain from the Battery to Harlem . . . and the ruffian for whom the East Side has become too hot, has only to step across town and change his name, a matter usually much easier for him than to change his shirt, to find a sanctuary in which to plot fresh outrages. The more notorious he is, the warmer the welcome . . .[22]

The complexion of the gangs, however, had been changing in several ways since the peace treaty between Monk Eastman and Paul Kelly in 1903. By 1912 both Eastman and Kelly had lost their former power, due to imprisonment, individual assassination attempts, and the growing strength of the reform movement. Their gangs had been broken up into factions, never to regain their former strength.

Eastman and Kelly, whose names were originally Osterman and Vaccarelli, were part of an ethnic shift in gang leadership. New gang leaders no longer pretended to be Irish. Other nationalities, particularly Jews and Italians, came to power within the gangs. Two of the three most important remnants of the Monk Eastman gang, for example, came under the leadership of Jack Sirocco, an Italian, and Big Jack Zelig, a Jew whose name was William Alberts. In time, Zelig's gang included such ambitious young thugs as Gyp the Blood, Lefty Louis, Dago Frank and Whitey Lewis, whose real names were, respectively, Harry Horowitz, Louis Rosenberg, Frank Cirofici and Jacob Siedenshner.

But by the time the Irish gangs relinquished some of their power to other nationalities, the fruits of gangsterdom were

[22] Ibid., p. 172.

considerably less bountiful. Compare the price list for crimes
quoted by the Whyos in the post Civil War period to the following
price list quoted by Big Jack Zelig.

Slash on cheek with knife	$ 1 to $ 10
Shot in leg	$ 1 to $ 25
Shot in arm	$ 5 to $ 25
Throwing a bomb	$ 5 to $ 50
Murder	$10 to $100

Killing and wounding were now much less profitable pas-
times; in fact, in some areas, a nice, clean, no-evidence-left
murder could be ordered for as little as $2.00.

One reason for these low prices was an over-supply of willing killers and maimers and thieves. But in the Hell's Kitchen
area it was due to the watchful eye of the New York Central
Railroad. For many years the various Hell's Kitchen gangs,
particularly the Gophers, had stolen freely from the freight cars
in the yards along Eleventh Avenue, and while the New York
Central had complained vigorously to the authorities, nothing
had been done.

The railroad finally took matters into its own hands and
hired a special force of guards to patrol the Eleventh Avenue
freight yards and depots. The guards were all highly trained and
many were former policemen who had quit the force in frustra-
tion at the coddling the gangs received from the politicians.
To a man, the New York Central guards went at their duties
with enthusiasm, clubbing every gang member who dared to
venture into their territory. When the gangs tried using guns
against the guards, they used guns, too, and with much greater
accuracy. Soon, the New York Central yards were recognized as
a completely lost source of revenue.

After this, the Gophers split into three factions, although
Irishmen maintained leadership of all three—Buck O'Brien,
Owen Madden, and an ineffective tough named Sullivan whose
territory was soon taken over by O'Brien and Madden. The divi-

sion of the Gophers was just one of the troubles besetting and upsetting the underworld community in New York:

> "By the latter part of 1913 . . ." wrote Herbert Asbury, "it is likely that there were more gangs in New York than at any other period in the history of the metropolis; their number and the ramifications of their alliances were so bewildering that of hundreds there now [1927] exists no more than a trace; they flashed into the ken of the police-man and the reporter and flashed out again like comets, leaving a gaseous trail of blood and graft . . . an area which in former years had been plundered exclusively by a single great gang became the haunt of innumerable small groups, which constantly fought each other, frequently strayed beyond their own domains, and robbed and murdered when-ever the opportunity for gain presented itself. Moreover, their organization was more elastic; there no longer existed the undying loyalty to the captain which had been such a distinguishing characteristic of the old-time gangs, and it was not unusual for a gangster to owe allegiance to three or four leaders at the same time, performing a different sort of thuggery for each. Throughout the city there were also a far greater number of independent thugs who bound themselves to a chieftain only for a definite campaign or for a specific blackjacking, stabbing or shooting assignment. The number of gangsters of this type continued to increase as decency invaded politics, and as the police became more honest and efficient and waged clubbing campaigns against the organized gangs." [24]

It was extremely difficult now to make a decent living through ordinary street crime. The police became tougher and tougher and the corrupt politicians, worried about their own futures in this era of political reform, were afraid to extend the same protection they had offered the gangs in previous years.

[23] Asbury, p. 331.
[24] Ibid., pp. 360–361.

For a short time labor union leaders as well as their opponents, the factory owners, showed signs of succeeding the politicians as the supporters of the gangs. In 1911, union leaders began hiring toughs to murder and blackjack strike breakers and to "persuade" workers who refused to join the union. The factory owners soon hired their own thugs to guard strike breakers. Within a few months, nearly every gang leader was on the payroll of either a union or a company, and blackjacking, stabbing, and brawling were common fare in labor-management relations. Once again, certain gang leaders commanded considerable power —Dopey Benny, Joe the Greaser, Little Rhody, Pinchey Paul,

Gangs sold their services to both labor unions and factory owners during strikes. This drawing by Winslow Homer pictures a clash that occurred during a railroad strike.   *Library of Congress*

and Billy Lustig. These gangsters were the best known of the period and all preferred to work for the labor unions; the employers had to settle for lesser toughs.

Dopey Benny was undoubtedly the most skillful and powerful of these five most important gang leaders. He would hire out the services of his henchmen for any purpose, and his gang soon gained the reputation of always having plenty of jobs. Attracted by the promise of constant work, many of the most ferocious gangsters in the city declared their loyalty to him. Even Joe the Greaser formed an alliance between his gang and Dopey Benny's and many members of smaller gangs left to join Dopey Benny. Finally, in desperation, these smaller gangs united in 1913, and declared war against Dopey Benny and Joe the Greaser.

From November 1913 to January 1914 the rival gangs battled whenever they met, although their fights were trivial compared to the great gang wars of the past. In January 1914, however, an innocent passerby, a court clerk with important political connections, was killed during a shoot-out between the gangs, and for the first time in the history of gangdom, all-out war was declared by the authorities against the gangs.

In November 1913, John Purroy had beaten the Tammany Hall candidate for the office of mayor. During his campaign he promised to put an end to police corruption and to the supremacy of the gangs. Once in office, he ordered his police commissioner to suppress the gangs at all costs and revoked an earlier, corrupt mayor's ban on the use of nightsticks by the police.

Within a year more than 200 of the most important gang leaders had been imprisoned. By 1916 the major gangs had been smashed. Some gangsters continued to work for the labor unions, but even the labor movement was cowed by the authorities' determination to end the wholesale violence that had wracked the city for years. Other gangsters pursued criminal activities on an individual basis, and as gang leaders were released from prison they were sometimes successful in gathering together the remnants of their old gangs and renewing former power.

By the middle 1920's the gangs were being spoken of in the past tense, and in the press frequent references were made to "the end of the gangs." In the prosperity and optimism of the post World War I era, it seemed perfectly realistic to believe that the gangs of New York were gone for good.

Another reason for this optimism, though not often mentioned publicly, was that the flood of immigrants that had washed over the country, particularly its northern cities, was reduced to just a trickle. The post-war period had seen a great amount of anti-foreign sentiment, not so much within the cities as outside them—in the rural areas of the South and West. This strong sentiment brought about a series of immigration laws between 1921 and 1924 that placed strict quotas upon the number of immigrants from Europe as well as from the Orient. Fewer foreigners would mean fewer problems—fewer poor, fewer criminals. Industrialization would continue, creating jobs for the immigrants already here, and with such opportunity perhaps they would pull themselves up out of the slums.

This is not what happened, of course. The demand for unskilled labor was much greater than the supply and so new sources of labor had to be found. The migration of blacks from the South and of Puerto Ricans from their island home began. Both groups headed for the industrial cities in the North. The movement was slow in the early 1920's but gained steadily during the decade, and eventually the "problem" of the foreigners would be replaced by the "problem" of the Negroes and Puerto Ricans.

And these were not the only problems. Bootlegging was gaining national attention. The Eighteenth Amendment prohibiting the sale of alcoholic beverages was passed in 1919 in an effort to curb drunkenness and alcoholism. It did not curb drunkenness and alcoholism, but it did provide a whole new range of illegal business possibilities and also began a new era for the gangs. Large bootlegging enterprises, speakeasies where illegal liquor was sold, cocktail waitress-prostitutes to serve customers —all were part and parcel of prohibition.

The Eighteenth Amendment was repealed in 1933, but the repeal came much too late to halt the steamrolling racketeering business. Organized crime came into its own during this period, the doors opened wide by the attempt to put all of America "on the wagon." The center of gang activity shifted to Chicago, where such names as Al Capone and Dutch Schultz became legend.

No other period of gang activity has been so widely publicized, from books to radio to televison to the cinema. And no other gang has been widely publicized as the Mafia.

Like the Chinese tongs, the Mafia did not originate in this country but was brought over from the homeland. It began in Sicily in 1282 as a secret society dedicated to the overthrow of the French occupiers of Italy. It was not the only such secret society; others, notably the Camorra in Naples, arose for the same reason. These secret societies were strong and greatly feared organizations, but their vitality depended almost solely upon anti-French activity. After the French left Italy, the secret societies degenerated. Although they remained alive for the next 700 years, by the middle of the nineteenth century they were little more than groups of families feuding with each other, not unlike the feuding mountain families of American folklore.

When Italians began to immigrate to America in the late 1880's and 1890's, they were beset with the same problems that had met other immigrant groups before them: alienation, discrimination, crowded tenement housing, unemployment, weakened family life, lack of community life. In New York, Sicilians settled in lower Manhattan and in Harlem, Neapolitans in Brooklyn. Such regional groupings naturally gave new life to the secret societies of the old country, the Mafia in lower Manhattan and Harlem, the Camorra in Brooklyn. The need was great for some sort of neighborhood authority, and the men who had belonged to secret societies in Italy reorganized to meet that need.

At first, their activities were quite legal, deciding disputes and otherwise helping their frightened, impoverished countrymen. However, it was not long before the secret societies abused

Italian immigrants maintain the traditions of the old country by celebrating the Feast of St. Rocco.

The Jacob A. Riis Collection, Museum of the City of New York

their influence in the communities. They charged neighborhood coal dealers, ice haulers, and shopkeepers for "protection." The money they got from their own countrymen was used to finance narcotics, gambling, and larger extortion enterprises.

As they grew more powerful, the racketeers became more and more organized. Positions within the societies were clearly defined, and rules of loyalty were absolutely rigid. The law of *omerta*, or silence, was ancient and iron-clad. Omerta went back to the beginnings of the secret societies, and it was continued in this country. The punishment for breaking this law was death, and there were ancient ways of letting the "squealer" know that he would die. One means was the receipt of a dead bird; another was being kissed by a leader. It was called the "kiss of death," and anyone who received it knew immediately that he would soon be assassinated.

Like the street gangs born in America, the organization of the Italian secret societies was very elaborate and they placed great importance on their rituals and ceremonies. Where the Mafia and Camorra differed from American born street gangs was in their taboos on distinctive dress and public actions. They were *secret* societies, and the code of secrecy was applied to every aspect of their existence. The members of the Mafia had no need for publicity.

By 1917 the secret societies had become large and powerful enough to extend their activities beyond their own neighborhoods and to come into conflict with each other and with other gangs. Periodically, there were gang wars over control of narcotics, gambling and extortion rackets in various areas of Chicago and New York, but not until the 1920's did the Italian secret societies, especially the Mafia, gain almost complete control of organized crime in America.

When the Volstead Act was passed, banning all hard liquor, the gangs of America immediately saw the possibilities of great profit from bootlegging liquor. Within two years, every gang in Chicago and New York and their surrounding suburbs was engaged in bootlegging as its major operation. Italian gangs, Polish gangs, Irish gangs, Jewish gangs—no gang bothered the others, and all got richer and richer. But after three years the gangs became greedy, and gang wars over control of bootlegging in various areas broke out often.

It was at this time that the Mafia, under Al Capone, gained control of the Chicago underworld. Capone, a Neopolitan, was not actually part of the Mafia. He had started with the Camorra in Brooklyn but had been sent for by a Mafia uncle in Chicago in 1909 and had succeeded to power when his uncle had retired. Capone had a genius for organization, and under his guid-

Under the Volstead Act, hard liquor, affectionately referred to as John Barleycorn, was not legally available. Its distribution was the making of the Mafia.   *RKO Radio Pictures, Inc.*

ance the Mafia seized control of bootlegging in Chicago. In 1928, by the age of 29, Capone was acknowledged the king of the Chicago underworld.

The gang wars continued throughout the late 1920's and into the 1930's. The St. Valentine's Day Massacre was widely publicized, but bombings and machine-gunnings became almost weekly occurrences on Chicago and New York streets. Violence was a way of life for the Mafiosi. The trouble was that too much violence was bad for business, and in New York a young Mafia lieutenant named Lucky Luciano decided it was time to end the fighting and get back to the business of making money.

The problem, in Luciano's eyes, was the Mafia leaders, whom he considered old and riveted to out-dated ways, and so he decided to get rid of these leaders. On the night of September 10, 1931, Luciano's men, in the largest and best orchestrated mass assassination in gang history, got rid of 40 old-time bosses around the country.

Immediately after that, Luciano began to institute the widereaching reforms that he had long felt the Mafia needed. He abolished the position of *Capo di tutti Capi,* or "Boss of Bosses," replacing it with a *Commissione,* or council, made up of bosses of the leading Mafia families across the country. Major decisions would thus be the responsibility not of one man but a group of men. He also introduced a system of "checks and balances" in regard to murders of gang members ordered by their

The notorious Mafia organizer Lucky Luciano.   *New York Daily News*

superiors. Henceforth, each family would have a *consiglieri,* or counselor, and before the murder of a "soldier" was ordered, the charges against him would have to be brought before the consiglieri for approval. In addition, Luciano refused to go along with either regional or ethnic rivalries, urging Neapolitans and Sicilians to work together and making pacts with such non-Italian leaders as Dutch Schultz and Meyer Lansky.

After a period of quiet under Luciano, the Mafia once again fell to bickering and in-fighting. Although the Volstead Act was repealed in the 1930's, gambling, extortion, narcotics and other illegal activities were large enough prizes to be fought over. It was not until the 1960's, however, that major changes occurred within the Mafia. At that time Joseph Colombo became boss of the largest Brooklyn Mafia family.

Colombo carried on the heritage of Lucky Luciano in trying to modernize the Mafia. The youngest boss in the country, he insisted that his men get involved in legitimate business as well as in the rackets and made a strong plea at meetings of the Commissione that other Mafia families do the same. He also promoted the younger men in his organization over the older men. But Joseph Colombo did more than that; toward the end of the 1960's he began to take some very bold and very dangerous steps that went far beyond "modernization."

During the 1960's there was a resurgence of pride in ethnic heritage. Groups that had for decades celebrated "the old ways" only in private now proclaimed them publicly. Suddenly, being "an American" was not as interesting or as prideful as being "Irish" or "German" or "Jewish." Members of the Italian community felt this resurgence of pride in their heritage, too, and among them was Joseph Colombo.

Colombo was tired of the image of Italians as gangsters—this may be one reason for his feeling that the Mafia should get into more legitimate businesses. He felt that Italians were discriminated against, and he decided to do something about it. He began to speak out, insisting that there was no Mafia, pointing with pride at the good things Italians had done. He founded the Italian-American Civil Rights League and led demonstrations against police stations and other institutions which he felt were guilty of discriminating against Italians. The law-abiding Italian community applauded Joseph Colombo; the Mafia bosses did not.

In the opinion of many of the other bosses, particularly the older ones, Colombo was breaking too many rules. The law of omerta was sacred to them, and Colombo was disregarding it completely. Although Mafia bosses had experienced much publicity over the years, none had sought it; in fact, they had shunned it at all costs. Colombo was actively seeking it.

On June 28, 1971, at the second annual Italian-American Civil Rights League Unity Day rally, Joseph Colombo was gunned down. Whether he was shot because he had talked too much or because of gang rivalries has not been conclusively proved, but the assassination attempt seemed to touch off a new round of gangland killings. The press attempted to compare these killings with the gang wars in Chicago in the 1920's and with other previous gang wars, but they were stretching the point. There would never again be that kind of wholesale violence in the underworld.

The Mafia has changed greatly since the late nineteenth century when frightened Italian immigrants in a strange land had renewed the bonds of their ancient secret societies. It began in this country for many of the same reasons that other gangs and groups formed. But there were major differences between the Mafia and American street gangs, and because of these differences it did not dissolve as most street gangs did. One difference was the strong tradition of loyalty and secrecy, which made it difficult for police and other government authorities to *find* the Mafiosi, and more difficult still to prove them guilty of crimes. Another was the organizational skill of some of its Chi-

cago leaders during Prohibition. In that era the Mafia wrested
control of bootlegging from other gangs and became a million-
dollar operation. Afterward, the demand for prostitution, gambling and drugs remained, and the Mafia simply shifted its
efforts back to those markets. Its control of the underworld was
never seriously challenged after Prohibition, so it continued to
prosper through crime.

Now, the Mafia has begun to go into legitimate business, its
bosses taking on ever greater respectability as "businessmen."
Deepening inroads into Mafia-controlled rackets are being made
by other ethnic criminal organizations, among them, the black
underworld. As Italian-Americans have become part of American society, Mafia influence in the Italian-American community
has become less strong. But despite these dangers to its existence, the Mafia lives on. After all, it can trace its beginnings
back to 1282, and in its permanency, in its size and in its
power, it has become an institution, and institutions seldom die.

Street gangs in the modern era

In this book, the era of the modern street gang is defined as the period beginning after World War II, and extending to the present time. It is distinguished from the preceding era in several ways: (1) the gang membership is younger (2) the nationality of the gang membership becomes primarily non-white —black, Hispanic, Mexican—although Italians, Irish and other white ethnic groups still make up a significant percentage (3) drugs become a greater and more publicized concern (4) gang activity tends to center around large-scale, well-organized street fighting resulting in death and injury to many of their members (5) fire arms and other lethal weapons are more readily available and more commonly used (6) their structure becomes more rigid, with titled, designated leadership, and groupings by age or federations with other groups (7) society becomes concerned with the gangs as a social problem and attempts to understand them, to work with them, to rehabilitate them.

The modern gang era shares in common with the preceding gang era the slum environment, worship of bravado, toughness, cleverness, love of publicity, the tendency to engage in acts "just for kicks," and many other characteristics. Herbert Asbury wrote of the nineteenth century gangs:

> . . . the gangster whose reign ended with the murder of Kid Dropper was primarily a product of his environment; poverty and disorganization of home and community brought him into being, and political corruption and all its attendant evils fostered his growth. He generally began as a member of a juvenile gang, and lack of proper direction and supervision naturally graduated him into the ranks of older gangsters . . . his only escape from the misery of his surroundings lay in excitement, and he could imagine no outlet for his turbulent spirit save sex and fighting.[25]

With minor changes, this paragraph could have been written by a sympathetic observer of gangs today.

As stated in Chapter I, anti-immigration laws in the 1920's reduced to a trickle the flow of Europeans and Orientals to America, and opened the way for considerable black immigration from the South to northern industrial centers. Even before the actual immigration laws went into effect, a shortage of European and Oriental workers had created job opportunities in northern cities. World War I had forced would-be immigrants to stay at home, and so from 1917 on, their places in the work force had to be filled.

Most black migrants came from the South but many also came from Jamaica, Barbados and other islands in the British West Indies. By 1930 the black population of New York, swelling from both sources, had risen from 91,709 in 1910 to 327,000.

The Depression in the 1930's slackened this movement. There were no job opportunities for newcomers with unemployment already high in northern cities. In a time of misery for all, blacks were most miserable.

[25] Asbury, pp. 127–128.

Then as World War II approached the economy recovered, and the migration from the South as well as the West Indies picked up. By 1950 there were 800,000 blacks in New York City, and the number was rising steadily. For the most part they were concentrated in Harlem, although there were many blacks in other areas, too.

Harlem had been "a community of great expectations" toward the end of the nineteenth century, a community of broad, treelined avenues and stately townhouses. It was expected to develop into an upper middle-class section. The fairly large numbers of Italians and blacks scattered throughout the area were treated as minor annoyances that would somehow, if ignored, go away. Exactly the opposite happened, however, for in the end it was the middle and upper middle-class inhabitants who went away.

The problem was over-speculation. In anticipation of elevated subway lines which would make the area accessible to the hub of the city, too many buildings were erected too early. Some were finished four or five years before the completion of the subway lines. Rents in the new luxury apartments were too high for the average citizens, and even after the subway lines were completed, there was no great rush northward to Harlem. Suddenly, the speculators were faced with tenantless buildings and creditors who demanded repayment of their loans. The only way the speculaters could recoup their losses was to sell at whatever price they could get or to reduce rents and lease to anyone willing to pay. Black and white realtors stepped in to buy the buildings, poor black tenants moved in, and by the 1920's Harlem was becoming a black neighborhood. Southern migrants filled the empty apartment houses, then overflowed them. Shrewd landlords broke up the large apartments into several small ones, taking little trouble to provide adequate sanitary facilities in the process. When the Depression came, the area was turning into a ghetto. Unemployment was rampant, blacks were the "last hired and first fired," and there was an over-all feeling of hopelessness.

A common sight in East Harlem today—crumbling tenements and vacant lots.
Robert Goldberg

With the advent of World War II jobs were plentiful again, but they came too late to stem the tide of poverty flowing through Harlem and by now, with the black population a visible and troublesome element, nothing could break down the barriers that the white community had erected around Harlem. The area couldn't have been riper for the sprouting of street gangs.

Similar seeds were being sown in other cities across the country. Harlem was by no means unique; but it was one of the first black ghettos. Another was the Lawndale section of Chicago:

> We've got . . . seventy thousand people in one square mile where there used to be only ten thousand. Until the fifties Lawndale was a middle-class Jewish neighborhood, but people panicked when blacks began moving in, and as

the Jews moved out, real estate brokers bought houses one week for fourteen thousand dollars and sold them to blacks the next week for twenty-six. The only way people could afford to live there was to divide up the houses and make apartments. A place is designed to hold just so many people, but in our hoods, everything gets jammed up. You have two or three families in one six-room apartment. When this was white, there was just one family in the same space.[26]

Meanwhile, another group of people was making its way to New York and certain other cities on the eastern seaboard. Like the southern blacks and the British West Indians, the Puerto Ricans were drawn to the mainland because they wanted to make a better life for themselves. Their island home was over-populated, causing widespread and chronic unemployment. And like black migration, Puerto Rican immigration began slowly after World War I when many jobs for unskilled workers were open. The ships which brought Puerto Ricans to the United States landed in New York, so naturally that is where the first Puerto Ricans settled, often within sight of the immigration processing center on New York's Lower East Side.

Immigration of Puerto Ricans continued slowly but steadily throughout the 1920's. With the Depression, it was reduced considerably. In fact, some Depression years saw more Puerto Ricans returning to their island home than leaving it. With World War II, however, immigration picked up again. Now commercial airlines had regular service between San Juan and New York. Like the shipping lines, the airlines were based in New York, and the immigrants who flew there were received warmly by the earlier immigrants who had established Puerto Rican communities in the city.

Between 1941 and 1956, over half a million Puerto Ricans arrived in the United States, and most of them settled in New York. There were Puerto Ricans living on the Lower East Side,

[26] David Dawley, *A Nation of Lords: The Autobiography of the Vice Lords.* Garden City, N.Y.: Doubleday, 1973, pp. 17–18.

in East Harlem which became known as *El Barrio,* which means "The District" or "The Neighborhood," in the South Bronx and in parts of Brooklyn. Like Harlem, these neighborhoods soon became slums, due to opportunistic landlords and discrimination which sealed off these areas from the white community. The Puerto Ricans encouraged this sealing off in some ways, preferring to keep their own culture and language rather than to try to mix into the larger society. The Puerto Rican areas were also ripe for gang activity.

Due in large measure to this huge influx of blacks and Puerto Ricans into northern cities, the post World War II period spawned the greatest era of youth gang activity in American gang history. As both the black and Puerto Rican communities began to grow, the old Italian, Jewish and Irish inhabitants became fearful that "the blacks were taking over" or "the Puerto Ricans were taking over." Young Italians, Jews and Irish heard their parents express these fears and took them as their own. Soon, among the youths, boundaries were strictly defined, with certain blocks "belonging" to Italians, some to Negroes, some to Irish, some to Puerto Ricans. The young Italians on one block would beat up any black youths who ventured onto their block, and, in retaliation, the friends of the blacks who had been beaten would beat up an Italian who attempted to pass through their area. Before long many of these groups of "neighborhood protectors" had organized themselves into fighting gangs, and by 1948 they dominated Harlem. Their power did not derive so much from their numbers, as from their ability to inspire fear— only a minority of Harlem teenagers belonged to fighting gangs. Gang members were sworn to revenge a hurt to one of their own. Their solidarity made them bold. Community residents, fearful of becoming targets of gang violence, did not support one another and were therefore vulnerable to further intimidation.

Some of the names of the gangs recalled the gang names

The Knifers, a gang of the early 50's, at a favorite hangout.
New York City Youth Board

of the nineteenth century: Beavers (Gophers), Avenue "L" Boys
(Bowery Boys). Others, more than in the nineteenth century,
made painfully obvious their need for self-esteem: Imperial
Counts, Dukes, Ambassadors, Viceroys, Bladesmen, Noble Eng-
lishmen, Enchanters. And still others revealed their ethnic
make-up: Baby Gent's Bambinos, the Latin Gents. As important,
if not more important than their names were their leather jackets emblazoned with gang emblems. The member with the
greatest artistic talent usually designed an emblem and then the
gang ordered patches made in the design. Girlfriends stitched
the patches to the backs of the black leather jackets, creating a
uniform in which one could walk proud—or scared.

A fighting gang of the 50's.
New York City Youth Board

Few gang members were brave enough to wear the jacket when they were alone and not on their own "turf." In the 1950's Christopher Rand wrote:

On the Lower East Side one often sees Puerto Rican boys in leather jackets with nickel stars on their shoulders as if they were generals. These jackets can be bought on Orchard Street for about fifteen dollars. The colored ones cost a few dollars more. They are usually made to order, in special colors and with special names on the backs, for clubs, baseball teams, and the like, and one hears that they are a mainstay of the gangs to which Puerto Rican and other slum boys belong. 'The gangs might even go out of existence,' a priest on the Lower East Side has told me, 'if their members couldn't buy those jackets. . .' " [27]

[27] Christopher Rand, *The Puerto Ricans.* New York: Oxford University Press, 1958, p. 14.

Mannerisms were also an important means of identification particularly to distinguish fighting gangs from non-fighting gangs.

While some gangs fought mostly to protect themselves and their block, other gangs went out looking for trouble, looking for fights. There were ways to tell fighting gangs from non-fighting gangs. When a gang decided to become a fighting, or "bopping" gang, its members immediately took on a different way of walking. A rhythmic gait, characterized by the forward movement of the head with each step, this walk was immediately recognizable. A gang member could tell whether another guy was a member of a "bopping" gang simply by watching the way he walked.

There were many "bopping" gangs in New York after World War II. Each was highly organized, with a president, a vice president, a warlord, and various other positions. They fought over "turf," over girls, and over whatever other reasons they could find. Among the more active gangs in East Harlem at this time were the Dragons, the Viceroys, the Turbans, and the Italian gang, the Red Wings. Typical of these fighting gangs was The Enchanters. Originating in East Harlem, this Puerto Rican gang had a total of seven divisions in the neighborhood by the early 1950's. Members were grouped according to age, which ranged from 9 to 20, in the Tiny Tots, the Mighty Mites, the Juniors, the Seniors, all the way up to The Enchanters. Later, branches were started in other parts of Manhattan as well as in the Bronx, Brooklyn, and Hoboken, New Jersey. As one former member recalled, "Man, The Enchanters weren't a gang—they were an organization." [28]

The brain behind the organization was 18 year-old Count Benny, who lived on 103rd Street. He hung out at the gang "headquarters," a candy store run by a woman called *La Vieja* (Old Lady), planning fighting actions and settling intragang disputes. The neighborhood candy store served the same purpose as the Five Points greengrocery over a century before—as an official meeting place and as a place simply to hang around.

One of the most brilliant ideas Count Benny had in La Vieja's candy story was to let other minority groups join The Enchanters. Although most of the members were still Puerto Ricans, the gang came to include some blacks and Italians. This way The Enchanters had access to areas that would normally be closed to them. It was quite a revolutionary step for most gangs remained strictly ethnic in their membership, Italian gangs pitted against Puerto Rican gangs, for example. A few years later, however, in 1957, a former Enchanter declared:

> The gangs used to be strictly according to whether you were a Puerto Rican or an Italian or something like that. Now, you hear all this talk about Italian gangs and Puerto

[28] Dan Wakefield, *Island in the City: The World of Spanish Harlem.* Boston: Houghton Mifflin, 1957, p. 126.

Rican gangs, but it's not all one way or the other. The Italian gang that's left up north has maybe twenty guys who are Puerto Ricans. It's not so much that stuff now as it is cliques—which clique is strongest. That's different than it was. Ten years ago I couldn't walk down 105th Street or I'd get it because I was a Spic.[29]

The Enchanters' chief rivals were the Dragons, another East Harlem gang. The Dragons were not as large a gang as The

[29] Ibid.

This Brooklyn gang of the late 50's is one of many that needed little excuse for a fight.   *Wide World Photos*

Enchanters, but they made up for it by making strong alliances with other gangs, among them, the Seminoles. An incident in 1955 showed how strong this alliance was. A 17 year-old youth, Feliciano, who had knifed a member of the Dragons in a fight over a 14-year-old girl, was in turn killed by a Seminole.

"I had just come back to 111th Street from school . . ." a member of the Seminoles told reporters, "when 'NoNo' Granna came running up and said, 'Johnny's been stabbed by Feliciano.' . . . We asked Victor Diaz (leader of the Seminoles) what to do and he said, 'Burn Feliciano.' . . . We found a bag . . . and put five blank slips of paper . . . in a bag and . . . wrote a B (for burn) on another slip and threw it in. Then we all drew slips. NoNo got the B but he punked out. He said, 'Count me out on this one.' Then 'Dillinger' Ramirez said he wanted to do the job and Victor said, 'You do it, Dillinger.' We went out on the street and Carmen Machuca came walking up . . . Victor told her to go . . . get the piece (a sawed-off .22 caliber rifle) . . . Then we talked about how to do the job. . . The others left and Victor and I walked down to 109th Street where some guys were fooling around an open hydrant. . . . Then Dillinger walked up and said, 'I already shot him.' Then we all gave each other some skin." [30]

This sort of revenge was required by the inflexible code of gang loyalty. It was from such incidents that the gangs drew their sense of pride, of "being somebody."

The gangs of the late 40's and 50's, like their predecessors in the nineteenth century, also engaged in brutal and cruel activities for no other reason than "just for kicks."

Well, the gang, they look for trouble, and then if they can't find no trouble, find something they can play around.

[30] "Teen-Age Terror on the New York Streets," *Life* (July 11, 1955), p. 33.

Go in the park, find a bum, hit him in the face, pee in his face, kick him down, then chase him, grab him and throw him over the fence.

—Boy, age 15 [31]

It should also be pointed out that gang members were not the only ones to engage in this sort of cruel, senseless activity. Groups of non-gang youths did so as well.

A year before the assassination of Feliciano, four Jewish youths in Brooklyn, Jack Koslow, Melvin Mittman, Jerome Lieberman, and Robert Trachtenburg, committed a senseless murder to which they confessed but which neither they nor anyone else was able to explain.

Because he was a little drunk, a man named Willard Menter was sleeping on a hard park bench. He was a black man; daytimes, he worked for $1 an hour running a blower in a dismal little burlap-bag mill. And the boys found him there.

They took off Menter's shoes while he snored and burned the soles of his feet with cigarettes—the way its done in the comic books. When Menter awoke with a yell, one of the boys hit him. Melvin Mittman said later that he liked to hit people. Then followed punching and kicking. Then they pulled Willie Menter to his feet and trudged with him down seven long, dark city blocks to the East River. . . There, in the shadows of the bridge their limp plaything was dumped into the river. (When it came to a showdown later, each boy minimized his own part in the crime.) [32]

[31] Kenneth B. Clark, *Dark Ghetto: Dilemmas of Social Power.* New York: Harper and Row, 1965, p. 3.
[32] Chester Morrison, "Could This Happen to Your Boy?" *Look* (November 2, 1954), p. 124.

Gang exploits made headlines in the press in the late 1940's and 1950's, perhaps because these years were a sort of "golden time" when, except for Korea, there was peace, and when, except for minor recessions, there was general prosperity. In general, the gangs liked it. Like their predecessors in the nineteenth century, publicity, good or bad, was actively sought. As one study in the 1950's reported:

> A prominent member of a gang in Chicago compiled [a] scrapbook filled with newspaper articles featuring his gang. . . . The names of the gang and of the individual members were underlined whenever they appeared in the articles. Gang boys at first are suspicious . . . about having newsmen follow them around in search of a story, as occasionally they do, but to the best of our knowledge reporters never experience prolonged difficulty and willing informants are usually at hand.[33]

Sometimes, the media interest in the gangs caused an upsurge in gang activity. A magazine spread, particularly one whose photographs showed gang members looking tough and cool, or a television documentary would immediately attract new members to the gangs featured, or would cause less active gangs to become more active in hopes of getting some publicity themselves. Probably the best case of media influence on gangs involved not street gangs but motorcycle gangs. In 1953 a movie called "The Wild One" was released. Starring Marlon Brando and Lee Marvin, the movie was about a motorcycle gang called the Black Rebels who invade a California town. The over-all story was not as important as the character portrayals of the "good outlaw," played by Marlon Brando, and the "bad outlaw," played by Lee Marvin, and their effect upon actual motorcycle gangs who saw the movie.

[33] James F. Short, Jr., ed., *Gang Delinquency and Delinquent Subcultures.* New York: Harper and Row, 1968, p. 20.

Marlon Brando as the "good outlaw" in "The Wild One."

"The Wild One" was a big hit among motorcycle gangs. The members of the Market Street Commandos, a California gang, each saw it four or five times; probably other gangs did also. And it is certain the movie influenced the Hell's Angels, who saw themselves as real-life Black Rebels. This California motorcycle gang had been formed by a group of World War II veterans and was becoming known on the West Coast for its drinking and brawling.

One would expect the Hell's Angels to have identified with Lee Marvin as the bad guy. His portrayal was much more true to life than Brando's. However, they identified with Brando, the confused hero. Hunter S. Thompson, who traveled with the Hell's Angels, explains it this way:

> They saw themselves as modern Robin Hoods . . . virile, inarticulate brutes whose good instincts got warped somewhere in the struggle for self-expression and who spent the rest of their violent lives seeking revenge on a world that done them wrong when they were young and defenseless.[34]

In the middle 1960's the media became fascinated with the Hell's Angels, chronicling in great detail two of their Labor Day motorcycle "runs" that had turned into riots and reprinting large sections of a report on the gang released by the California Attorney General. The press gave the gang more publicity in six months than it had in all the 15 years of its previous existence. As Hunter Thompson wrote:

> The whole scene changed in a flash. One day they were a gang of bums, scratching for any hard dollar . . . twenty-four hours later they were dealing with reporters, photographers, free-lance writers and all kinds of showbiz hustlers talking big money. By the middle of 1965 they were firmly established as all-Amercan bogeymen.[35]

[34] Hunter S. Thompson, *Hell's Angels: A Strange and Terrible Saga*. New York: Random House, 1966, p. 67.
[35] Ibid., p. 40.

A rash of gang movies like "Devils Angels" (pictured above) came out in the 50's and 60's. Many gangs in turn tried to live up to their movie image.

Although this example of media influence concerns motorcycle gangs, the amount of publicity the Hell's Angels received did have an effect upon urban street gangs. The street gangs did not identify with the Angels themselves—the Angels were considerably older and they were white—but they did identify with the image of toughness and bravado and with the all-important attention which that toughness and bravado had brought the Angels with the help of the media. Even now, though media coverage and thus the influence of motorcycle gangs has waned, members of Puerto Rican gangs in New York declare that owning a motorcycle is their ultimate goal.

While street gangs wanted all the publicity they could get, they often scoffed at the media portrayal of their world. Those who knew laughed at the perceptions of those who did not know.

"People see these movies and books about gangs and get to thinking that's the way it is," said one street gang member in the 1950's. "And most of it's phony. Just like this T.V. play we saw . . . about a gang, it could never have happened . . . they had some gang that wanted to take care of a kid, and so they dressed him up in their gang jacket and set him into the territory of an enemy gang and the enemy gang saw the kid and beat him up. Well, you know, there's no gang that'd make a guy dress in their jacket when he wasn't a member—it'd ruin the honor of the gang. They'd just take care of the kid themselves, that's all.

And lots of these stories in magazines and books, they usually have some racketeer who comes along and sells them guns . . . like it's that one guy who turned 'em bad. Hell. It's never like that. If a gang wants pieces, it gets pieces—it gets 'em all kinds of ways from all kinds of places. It's not just one guy coming along and selling them the idea himself." [36]

Pieces—guns. After World War II their use among the gangs became widespread. Even in the nineteenth century guns had been available, but the fighting gangs had preferred the direct physical contact of fists, heels, brass knuckles, and black-jacks. In the early years after World War II the fighting gangs also tended to rely on bicycle chains and clubs and broken bottles. But then something happened, and guns became all-important.

"Right after the war," a former gang member recalls, "I remember I was just a little kid and guns first started showing up a lot, in the open. At first it was a real big deal. A guy would pull a gun in the street and everyone out on the block would scatter. Maybe it wasn't even loaded, maybe you couldn't hit a thing with it; all you had to do was pull a gun. Then, people got used to 'em, and after awhile it got

[36] Wakefield, p. 142.

so a guy pulled a gun and another guy would just stand and ask him, 'Well, you going to use that or not? You better use it or put it away.' That's the way it got to be. That's why now (in 1957) there's none of this waving a gun around and watching people run. You got to use it or put it away." [37]

The gangs used their guns, as well as their knives and other weapons, and a seemingly endless series of gang wars occurred in the late 1950's and early 1960's. Newly-formed youth agencies and youth boards, based upon the idea that the gangs were a side-effect of the diseases of the ghetto, poverty, and

[37] Ibid., pp. 142–143.

Unaware of the arms build-up to come, a plainclothesman grimly divests this rumble-bound gang of their weapons—studded belts.

New York Daily News

racism, attempted to bring about truces and to work in other
ways with the teenagers. But these efforts didn't help much. Like
a series of explosions, each triggered by the other, gang violence
flared in one part of New York after another:

> At first, the Sportsmen, mostly Negro, and the Forsyth
> Street boys, mostly Puerto Rican, breached a three-year
> truce to launch a deady rumble in Manhattan's East Side.
> Next, violence flared in Brooklyn and in the Bronx, and in
> Jamaica, where the Chaplains, Sinners, Bishops and Chey-
> ennes fought to the death for "territorial rights." Over the
> weekend, the West Side of midtown Manhattan erupted.
> The week's toll in New York City's interminable teen-age
> gang wars:
>
> —Four dead.
> —At least fifteen hospitalized with serious knife, gun-
> shot, or bludgeon wounds.
> Two of those slain were 16; the third, a 15 year-old
> girl; the fourth, only 14.[38]

By the early 1960's, a new phenomenon had presented itself—female "bopping" or "jitterbugging" gangs. There had always been girl affiliates of the boys' gangs, waiting on the boys,
carrying messages for them, acting as their girlfriends. Often a
girl was the reason a gang war started. An improper glance from
a member of another gang could touch off a battle over her
honor or love. But by the early 1960's some of the girls had become dissatisfied with being merely affiliates and had formed
their own gangs, imitating the boys' fighting habits and frequently out-doing the boys in viciousness.

The girls organized mugging expeditions and shoplifting
sprees, crashed parties, got drunk on cheap wine, smoked marijuana and sniffed glue. In 1961 the New York City Youth Board
Commissioner had told a Senate subcommittee on juvenile delinquency:

[38] "Massacre in New York," *Newsweek* (September 7, 1959), p. 32.

"These girls are catalytic agents for conflict and violence. They will do anything to please the boy gang members, from carrying weapons, rumors and narcotics to outright promiscuity. They participate in petty theft, out-of-wedlock pregnancies and use alcohol and narcotics excessively." [39]

Often the girl gangs were attached to the boys' gangs, calling themselves the Avenger Debs, the Young Martyr Debs, the Dagger Debs, etc. They dressed like the boys, in tight pants and bulky jackets. The Dagger Debs affected ankle high boots and wound red bandanas tightly around their heads.

In the early 1960's the Dagger Debs' leader was Rena, a bright and imaginative girl who was fiercely possessive of Chips, the war lord of the Daggers. Rena organized many of her gang's fighting expeditions against girls who had looked at Chips in the wrong way. She was on probation for beating up a girl who had made eyes at Chips, she was pregnant by the 16-year-old Chips, she was angry, defiant, deeply in trouble, and she was 12 years old. The Youth Board could not say exactly how many girls like Rena there were in New York City, but in 1961 the Board itself was in touch with some 6,000 of them.

The New York City Youth Board and other agencies like it represented a totally new way of dealing with gangs. Before World War II the only city department that had dealt with the gangs had been the police. Various private groups had operated settlement houses and orphanages which tried to reach the children of the poor, but their work was never directed at gangs in particular. And those settlement houses and community centers which did want to bring the gangs into their programs found that their activities were only disrupted by the gangs, that the programs they offered were not designed for teenagers whose entire lives were street-oriented. Obviously, private agencies were not the answer.

[39] Kitty Hanson, "Teeners Run Wild in Theft, Dope, Sex," New York *Daily News* (August 21, 1962), p. 26.

A youth worker mediates a truce between rival gangs.
New York City Youth Board

Nor were police methods of dealing with the gangs the answer. In the nineteenth century, a massive campaign to wipe out the gangs would have been possible, but by the middle of the twentieth century it was not. After World War II, America was exhausted from fighting and violence. The nation had had enough of war. It did not, now, want war in its own cities. Then, too, by the middle 1940's, America had come to have a different view of its poor and disinherited. Psychology and sociology had come into their own as accepted, valid areas of study, and Americans were realizng more and more the effects that poverty and discrimination and ghetto life had upon human beings. Society now wanted to understand gangs and work to reform them rather than to destroy them.

In the middle 1940's a new approach to the gang was being tried in a number of large cities by voluntary agencies or individuals. Basically it involved the introduction of a neighborhood program of community organization and participation. Workers were sent out to make contact with the street gangs, to establish relationships with them, to become accepted by them and, once accepted, to try to redirect the gang members' anti-social behavior into socially-acceptable paths. The philosophy of the New York City Youth Board, as set forth in 1950, expresses well the philosophy of the general society in its new approach to the youth gang problem:

1. Participation in a street gang or club, like participation in any natural group, is a part of the growing-up process of adolescence. . . Within the structure of his group the individual can develop such characteristics as loyalty, leadership and community responsibility.

2. Some street clubs or gangs, as a result of . . . family disorganization, economic insecurity, . . . discrimination, poor housing, lack of recreational and educational facilities, emotional maladjustments . . . have developed patterns of anti-social behavior, the most widely known of which is street fighting. . .

3. While the protection of the community at times necessitates the use of repressive measures in dealing with the anti-social street clubs or gangs, these methods do not bring about basic changes in attitude or behavior.

4. Street club members can be reached and will respond to sympathy, acceptance, affection and understanding when approached by adults who possess those characteristics and reach out to them on their own level.[40]

[40] Report of "The Brooklyn Detached Worker Project," September 13, 1950, New York City Youth Board, *Reaching the Fighting Gang*. New York: New York City Youth Board, 1960, pp. 5–6.

Many youth workers had been gang members themselves once and knew first hand the frustrations of ghetto life. Their job was a difficult one. It took courage and perseverance to approach hostile and suspicious gang members. But workers achieved some success in averting violence and steering individuals into job training programs and away from gang involvement. The street workers risked their safety in arranging truces between warring gangs and some paid for their efforts with their lives.

A comparatively large body of literature resulted: books and studies on gangs, on the various methods of working with them, on case studies, on successes and failures. Street gangs and society's attempts to deal with them were dissected and redissected, evaluated and reevaluated. On paper, the street gang

A youth worker makes contact—the first step on the long road to winning a gang's confidence.   *New York City Youth Board*

"problem" was licked, although in reality there were many weaknesses in the programs for gangs. The greatest weaknesses were not the fault of the programs themselves. They were due to society, to the continuing poverty and discrimination, to the ghettos, to inequality of opportunity, to all the problems that fertilized the soil from which the gangs sprang.

In the late 1950's and early 60's, in New York and in many other cities the gang "problem" suddenly appeared to be "solved," but its "solution" was not the work of the New York City Youth Board and its counterparts in other affected cities, but of the street gangs themselves. The future would show, however, that in many ways the gang problem was not really "solved" at all, but simply turned into another problem.

Anger, defiance, fighting, killing—by the middle 1950's the gangs had become a means of terror to the gang members themselves as well as to outsiders. An incredible tension gripped the ghettos of New York and other major cities, and it was felt perhaps most keenly by gang members. You *had* to be tough, you *had* to revenge every slight, you *had* to carry a piece or a knife, and you *had* to use it or someone else would use theirs on you. You had to be on your guard all the time, you could never relax. By the time you were 16 you knew too much, had done too much, had seen too much, and the strain was too much. You had to reduce the tension.

There were different ways to accomplish this. One way for an individual gang member was to quit the gang, go back to school or find a job. But it was a difficult step. Some gangs had an unwritten law that once a youth was a member he could never quit; if he tried to leave he would be found and severely beaten. Even those youths whose gangs would allow them to quit, sometimes found it impossible to make the break. The gang, after all satisfies a basic need—it offers a sense of belonging to its members; a gang is a family, its headquarters, home. Leaving the gang was often like leaving family and home to face alone the harshness of the ghetto world, and many gang members changed their minds and stayed rather than face this loneliness.

Another way to reduce the tension was for a gang as a whole to forswear violence and "go social." This was a big step also, and it was not usually taken by powerful, cohesive gangs. Most often those gangs who chose to go social did so because they were no longer an effective gang group.

One of the gangs that chose to go social was The Enchanters, and the story of their change is typical of that of other gangs who made the same choice. By the late 1950's this once powerful and greatly feared gang was weak and fearful itself. Its former leaders were either dead, in prison, or in narcotics treatment centers, and no strong new leaders had come along to take their place. All around them were powerful rival gangs and, knowing they were no longer any match for their rivals, The Enchanters chose to go social in order to survive. As a gang that had given up fighting, as a social club, they would not be bothered by the other gangs.

The first step toward going social was to change their name. The name, The Enchanters, stood for fighting, and if they were to give up fighting they had to have a new name. They decided upon The Conservatives after many stormy sessions which saw some members walk out and join other fighting gangs and many of the girls bitterly oppose the complete disposal of the old name. Many of the girls had dated Enchanters who were now in jail or dead or in the hospital and they felt that respect should be paid to them. They proposed that the new name be "The Conservative E's." The girls may have had different, unspoken reasons for being against a complete break with the past. The Enchanters had fought many battles over the honor of their girls, and the girls had felt very important. If the new Conservatives gave up fighting altogether, the girls would not be as important. Finally, however, those who sincerely wanted to go social prevailed and The Enchanters officially became The Conservatives.

Adopting a new name, though important, was a minor step. The major break with the past came when the members of the gang gave up their guns. This was also the most dangerous step,

A gang member burns his jacket—part of the ritual of "going social" in the 70's.

New York Daily News

because they were depending upon the other gangs to respect their decision. If the other gangs did not, they were powerless to defend themselves. Except for one incident with the rival Dragons right after The Conservatives had given up their guns, the gangs tended to respect their decision and leave them alone.

The Conservatives found a clubhouse, held weekly meetings and charged dues. On Saturday nights they played records and danced. But it took more than a clubhouse and weekend dances to keep the gang members from getting into the troubles of the old days. Their name had been changed but not the overcrowded tenements, the teeming streets, the boredom, the sense of "being nobody." It was a test of will every day, and some couldn't make it. They joined other fighting gangs who scoffed at the idea of going social, or, they took the other way to escape the tension, they turned to drugs.

From a 1962 newspaper article:

"Getting high" is one of the primary goals of kids who live on the city streets, and they use everything from liquor or marijuana or heroin to get that way. Some of the girls have even tried the boys' latest "kick," sniffing model airplane glue in a bag.[41]

Wine made a guy feel like he could do anything; it gave him courage. With four or five pints of wine in him, he could fight like nobody else. Before a gang fight, most of the members of the opposing gangs would get high.

"You didn't become a better fighter, but you're faster with the alcohol," a Chicago Vice Lord said. "You might chop a cat's head off with that alcohol, but if you go fight him sober, you might hit him with one punch and the cat is laying down and you couldn't even kick him any more. If you're full of alcohol you can stomp him all day long and think nothing of it."[42]

[41] Kitty Hanson, "Youth Board Helps—Some," New York *Daily News* (August 23, 1962), p. 3.
[42] Dawley, p. 74.

Marijuana, on the other hand, made a guy feel so rational that he couldn't see the point in fighting. It made him more alert, sensitive to sounds, to lights. That was good, too, because he could avoid getting into a senseless fight.

Heroin made a guy forget everything, put him in a bubble floating above the teeming, filthy, ghetto streets. In the 1950's and early 60's, although heroin users were not frowned upon by the gangs and were included in gang activities where possible, the fighters were against the use of heroin. After all, once someone got hooked on it, he spent most of his time hustling to get the dope; he didn't have time for gangs or even parties. Nevertheless, heroin became king in the ghetto, and it became king by riding on the shoulders of fear.

It was a vicious circle. A guy joined a gang out of fear. He fought and he killed and he was arrested and jailed and his body became scarred, and suddenly he was older and he realized that life meant something different to him now than when he was 14 or 15 or 16. He wondered how he'd managed to come through it all without being killed or maimed himself, and once he started wondering he started wondering if the next time wouldn't be his time. But he couldn't get out of the circle. He had a "rep," and there were a thousand guys out there waiting to challenge him and earn a "rep" of their own. Wine made him accept every challenge; marijuana made him aware of every challenge. Only heroin made him forget.

Of course maintaining a "rep" was only one of the many pressures that turned gang members to drugs. Heroin was taken by non-gang members as well, and for non-gang members and gang members alike it provided escape from conditions that were no longer bearable. What these pressures were is a complex question, and the reasons for heroin addiction were different for each addict. Poverty, discrimination, violence, hopelessness, all the facets of ghetto life that had caused gang members to join their gangs in the first place were responsible. For those who became hooked on heroin, gang membership had failed to provide a solution to ghetto life.

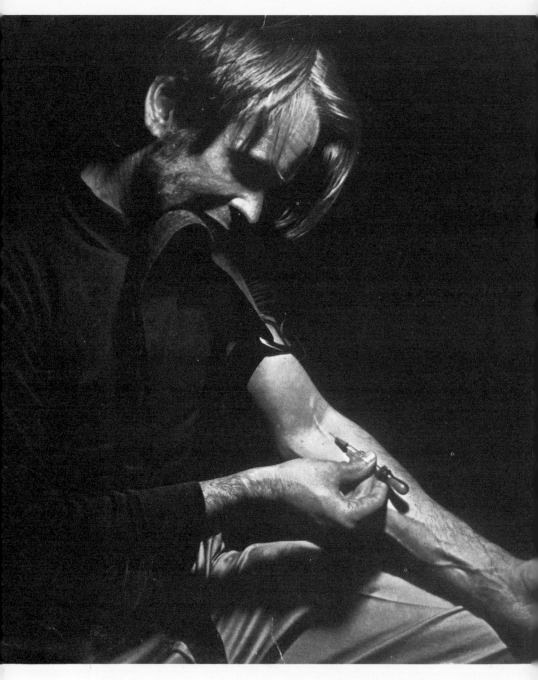

Many gang members in the late 50's turned to heroin only to find that addiction brought even more overwhelming problems.

Addiction Services Agency

It happened in New York first. Later, it would happen in Philadelphia and Chicago and Los Angeles, the other three gang capitols. By the early 1960's, authorities were beginning to see that when there was more drug use, there was less gang violence. The drug pusher had not only pushed drugs into the ghetto, he had also pushed the gangs out. Some authorities even went so far as to "credit" drugs for solving the gang problem. In Detroit, the police department's gang unit changed its name and went on to handle other matters. There had been strong political pressure to bring an end to gang violence, for it had been sensationalized in the press and had terrified respectable citizens outside the ghettos, even though the majority were never directly affected by it. But there was little political pressure to bring about an end to the violence heroin was causing in the ghettos. After all, it was just another "ghetto problem;" it hardly rated extensive news coverage. At first, it did not directly affect respectable citizens who may have hoped the ghetto would destroy itself.

New headlines hit the newspapers in the early 1960's; America shifted its attention to the civil rights movement. It was largely southern-based, this new movement, and at first it was not expected to have much effect on northern cities. But it proved to have a major effect throughout the country, and mostly because of television. When civil rights marchers were set upon with fire hoses and cattle prods, when civil rights workers were beaten and jailed, the actual events were often broadcast, live, on television. Northern blacks saw a racism more blatant than even they had imagined existed.

The urban ghetto riots of the middle 1960's occurred, in part, because the ghetto residents rejected as ineffective the nonviolence of the civil rights movement and opted for violence to show the system where the people of the ghetto stood. In Harlem, Newark, Detroit, Chicago, Watts, and other cities, the summers brought looting, burning, and pitched battles between ghetto residents and police. Ghetto youth participated in these riots, but not as gangs. Like the youth during the draft riots in the

1860's, they acted as part of the mob, caught up in the frenzy of destruction.

When the ghettos cooled, when the smoke cleared, new groups were born, not "gangs" as we have defined them, but groups of young people with a new interest and shrewdness in politics—the politics of confrontation, the politics of power. They carried guns and were willing to engage in violence, if necessary, but these new groups were not interested in violence for its own sake. They were interested in "helping the people," "helping the community." They were interested in stopping police brutality, in getting landlords to make ghetto tenements livable, in getting better sanitation service, in starting free programs to

A Harlem street after a long hot summer of rioting and looting.

New York Daily News

feed hungry children, in pushing drugs out, in frightening the larger society just enough to make it give up some power.

The Black Panthers arose in Oakland, California, a suburb of San Francisco in 1968; the Young Lords, a Puerto Rican gang, in East Harlem in the early 1970's; the Black Muslims who had formed in Chicago in the 1940's gained national prominence in the 1960's because of the forceful leadership of Malcolm X. All three groups opened chapters in other cities; other community groups followed their example. Although these local groups did not make headlines, like the Panthers, Muslims, and Young Lords, they too had a definite program to get the community off drugs, to convince their older brothers and sisters and those who protected the pushers that heroin was doing the system's job, that it was just another weapon of racism.

The Black Muslims differed in many ways from the Black Panthers and the Young Lords. The Black Muslim movement was based on a religion, upon separatism, and upon black independence much more than on politics. Basically, they left whites alone, and after a time whites left them alone.

The Panthers and Young Lords, however, believed in confrontation, and thus they were relatively short-lived as a political force. The picture on millions of television screens across the country of armed Panthers marching into the Capitol building in Sacramento to protest pending gun control legislation sent shivers down the spine of the system. Not long after that, shootouts between Panthers and police became commonplace, and the three major Panther leaders, Huey Newton, Eldridge Cleaver and Bobby Seale, were either imprisoned, caught up in endless court cases, or forced to leave the country. Whatever power they had briefly enjoyed was effectively neutralized. The system also struck back at the Young Lords and other potentially powerful and thus potentially dangerous groups.

Meanwhile, the new racial consciousness was having an effect on the activity of local street gangs. Gangs that had been involved in fighting or going social suddenly wanted to become involved in the community.

On New York's Lower East Side, a chiefly Puerto Rican gang called the Spartican Army, was typical of this new feeling. The gang decided to give up fighting ways and to become a constructive group working for change. They decided that it was their destiny to help the community, to rid the ghetto of crime and drugs, to help their people help themselves. How they were going to accomplish their goals, they did not know.

At this same time, in Washington, President Johnson was launching his War on Poverty, setting up federal agencies to deal with the urban ghetto and to work for social change. Hundreds of millions of dollars were earmarked for the rebuilding of riot-scarred inner cities, for job training, for antipoverty programs of every type and description.

Buoyed by Washington's idealism, local and state governments, private agencies and huge corporations began their own antipoverty programs. In the ghettos, groups were organized to take advantage of the flowing monies. The Spartican Army took a different stance. At this time, money did not interest them as much as support and the good will of the community. They wanted it made known that they had reformed and that they had, as a former fighting gang, a unique knowledge of the problems of youth in the ghetto and how to deal with those problems.

Members of the gang began to speak wherever they would be heard. They did not speak so much about how they had reformed as about their intentions to rid the streets of crime and drugs and to do so on their own. They were against charity, they said, insisting that charity never really helped anyone. They were also against conventional social service and youth development programs because they were run by adults and did not offer young people a voice in planning and directing the programs. They talked about the programs they planned to initiate, without funds or help from any outside sources. They impressed their audiences wherever they spoke, and they received extensive coverage in the press.

Their fame increased after they changed their name. In his book *The Gang and the Establishment*, Richard W. Poston chronicles the gang's development in great detail, including how the name change came about:

> One night they got into an especially vigorous discussion about the federally supported antipoverty agencies on the Lower East Side, how little the government knew about the realities of life in the ghetto, and the Great Society of President Johnson. With Charlie leading them on, the criticism grew to a roar. In the heat of the conversation, Chino suddenly shouted out, "We are the *real* Great Society."
>
> "That's it, that's it!" thundered Charlie, jumping to his feet. "The Real Great Society. That's what we are." [43]

The Real Great Society, or RGS, as it came to be known, rose to national fame; yet, in reality, it was little more than a myth. In the first place, it had only about half-a-dozen active members. It was these few who traveled to the speaking engagements. Although they did have meetings and sponsor activities at their apartment headquarters on New York's Lower East Side, many of the street youths who were drawn into the activities left because the apartment was so crowded that there was no room for them.

According to RGS, it was these overcrowded conditions that finally caused the group to go against its original rejection of outside funding as "charity." The group's outside counselors (there were more and more as RGS fame increased) urged the boys to apply for a grant from the federal Office of Economic Opportunity (OEO). They would use the money for larger and better physical facilities in which to carry out their programs.

[43] Richard W. Poston, *The Gang and the Establishment.* New York: Harper and Row, 1971, p. 37.

The group consented, but insisted in their application for the grant that there be no strings attached to the money. They wanted their programs to be directed entirely by RGS and its chosen counselors. Specifically, the program was to offer remedial basic education, vocational training and job placement, small business development, an instructional-materials center, a storefront library, and a day care center that would provide a wide range of services for preschool children. The amount requested for a two-year program: $2,450,000. The sum seems staggering given that the group was "against charity," and it is probable that their outside counselors set the figure.

The OEO turned the proposal down, but the RGS was not as disappointed as might have been expected. After all, hadn't they done something unheard of? A bunch of New York gang kids asking the government for two and a half million dollars! The boys were beginning to feel their power, but they had not yet lost sight of their idealistic goals.

Undiscouraged, the RGS counselors began to apply for grants from private foundations. They asked the Vincent Astor Foundation for $150,000 to start three new businesses and a neighborhood day care center. Early in 1967 they were informed that the Astor Foundation would award them a grant of $15,000.

Suddenly, the RGS had more money than it had ever had before. Suddenly, it had money to finance what they had only dreamed about before. They formed the Real Great Society, Incorporated. Of the $15,000, $9,000 went into the opening of a nightclub called the Fabulous Latin House; $3,000 went into the opening of The Leather Bag, which sold leather goods; and $3,000 went to establish the neighborhood child care service, known as the Visiting Mothers. Profits from these three ventures were to go into an account for new businesses.

Within a year all three projects had folded and the entire $15,000 had been spent. Lack of business knowledge and poor money management were the chief reasons for the failure. The boys would have liked nothing better than to have made the

AN OPEN LETTER

FROM

THE REAL GREAT SOCIETY

What can you expect from a group of young men from the Lower East Side who fought each other, fought other people, robbed them-- even tried to kill them--and sometimes went to jail?

I'll tell you what you can expect from them. You can expect them to wonder, to dream, "Is there anything else for me? What's on the other side of the wall? Can the things we speak about ever become a reality?"

You can even expect some of these young men to take the plunge--the plunge into trying to make a dream become a reality.

In 1964, a group of kids made that plunge. We call ourselves the Real Great Society. We have come a long way, but we are making the effort to go even further.

What is the Real Great Society? A group of people who believe that the individual has to really be considered as just that--an individual. We begin with the basics, so that before anything else, people will know how to work with each other. Originally, the Real Great Society started with Puerto Ricans. But we soon found out that if it's a Real Great Society we want to create, we are going to have to work with other people.

So we're working with others, as long as they realize that we all have something to offer. As Chino, our president, says, "Every man is not equal. Every man is great!"

In an open letter the Real Great Society's president, Carlos "Chino" Garcia, informs the public of the group's philosophy.

businesses work, but they learned that running a successful business took more than just desire.

Several months before the projects had folded, however, the RGS and its counselors had decided to return to the Astor Foundation with another proposal, this time for a summer educational program to be called the University of the Streets. Twenty-five thousand dollars was asked for, and since at that time all three of the operations financed by the first grant were in operation and, according to their publicity, going great, they got the money.

The University of the Streets opened in the summer of 1967, and from the start it received great publicity. Within its first three weeks of operation, 800 people signed up and during the summer its enrollment grew to more than 1,600. Hundreds of volunteers had offered their services, and classes ranged from preparation for high school equivalency tests to literature and philosophy, language, social problems, black and Puerto Rican history, karate, and radio and television repair.

Because the University was so popular, RGS counselors urged a new application to the OEO for federal funds. Meanwhile, basic operating expenses were paid with numerous small grants from small, private foundations. RGS got these grants because of the success that summer of the University of the Streets. That success, however, was not as great as it appeared. Although the University was intended for the local community residents, over 75% of its enrollment that summer was made up of white middle-class young people who had flocked to the East Village for a New York summer. The building that housed the University was located near the East Village, and naturally these young people used its facilities. At the end of the summer these young people went back to school, or moved on, and most of the volunteers, who were college teachers and students, went back to school as well. The number of courses offered by the University dropped, and its enrollment dropped to about 200. In reality, then, the University had reached only about 200 people from the community. Unphased, the RSG added to its list of arguments for an OEO grant that they needed money to reach more people in the community.

The University received the OEO grant, but not entirely on its or on the RGS's own merits. In some measure, the grant was made because of something in which the RGS and the University were not even involved. It happened that the summer of 1967 saw the worst outbreak of ghetto rioting yet, and the nation braced for more to come. Rioting did not occur in New York that summer and RGS claimed some credit for that. Whether or not this was deserved, suddenly the Real Great Society and its University of the Streets were seized upon, perhaps desperately, as a model—a way to calm the violence and also a dramatic solution to many of the ills which caused the violence.

Suddenly, in cities across the country, and particularly in Washington, the Real Great Society and its programs were on everyone's lips. As Richard Poston recalls:

> This story of spontaneous action by traditionally delinquent youth gangs, supported by substantial financing from wealthy private organizations and by the federal government, was in itself extraordinary enough. But beyond that I began to realize that what I had encountered was a growing mood among individuals and institutions in the field of grant-making to look upon urban street gangs as proper recipients of large sums of public and private money. . . . Underlying this . . . mood . . . was this simple theme: Positive change within the ghetto must be self-motivated and internally directed, and as was being illustrated on the Lower East Side, youth gangs were a prime source for this motivation and direction. . . With this kind of recognition, street gangs across the nation, usually regarded by the police as bands of hoodlums, could become bridges of understanding and cooperation between alien worlds—the ghetto and the larger society. . . . I had never

heard anything quite like it. . . This, it seemed to me, was one of the most significant social phenomena yet to emerge out of the urban despair of the sixties, which if sufficiently cultivated could become a major preventive for such despair in the seventies and beyond.[44]

Although the Real Great Society was the best known street gang to become community action-minded, they were not an isolated phenomenon. Other gangs in other cities also became advocates of self-help. In October of 1967, RSG invited these gangs to a conference in New York. The leaders who accepted the invitations were chiefly from New York, although Milwaukee, Washington, and San Francisco were also represented. There a new organization was born, Youth Organizations United (YOU), and plans were made for other conferences, at which more members would be recruited. Funding was gotten from private sources as well as from the Coalition for Youth Action of the Department of Labor; YOU was incorporated and a Washington office established. Feelers were sent out to large gangs in various cities, among them, the Conservative Vice Lords, a predominantly black gang from Chicago.

The Conservative Vice Lords, initially, were not interested. They were too busy trying to get funding for their own programs. A $15,000 grant had come through from the Rockefeller Foundation. That was enough to open an office and get some programs started, but by late March 1968 leaders of the Conservative Vice Lords were in Washington looking for federal grants. It was there that they were pursuaded by RGS to join YOU.

The Lords assumed the responsibility for recruiting new gang members in the Midwest, although the Lord leaders did not actually do the traveling and recruiting; they felt they didn't have the time. Thus, they hired Warren Gilmore, 36, who had joined their organization a few months earlier, to be recruiter. Gilmore did an excellent job, and he is to be credited for attract-

[44] Ibid., pp. x, xi.

Warren Gilmore, president of Youth Organizations United, in the organization's Washington headquarters.   *Wide World Photos*

ing many of the 120 delegates to the national YOU conference held in East St. Louis, Missouri, in the middle of May, 1968.

Fifty groups from 22 cities sent delegates to the conference. The Midwest, thanks to Gilmore, was heavily represented; the East was represented by Massachusetts, New York, Pennsylvania, and Washington, D.C.; the West, by San Francisco, Los Angeles, and Sacramento; the South, by New Orleans. The majority of delegates ranged in age from 18 to 25, although a few were in their 30's and a couple were past 40. About 90% were black, the remaining 10% being Puerto Ricans and Mexican-Americans, with a few Chinese, Japanese, and American Indians. They did not know each other and they did not trust each other. Initial displays of independence and toughness threatened to ruin the conference. Unity prevailed in the end, however, but not in the direction the RGS had envisioned.

The Conservative Vice Lords outside their headquarters.
The Vice Lords by R. Lincoln Keiser, Holt, Rinehart and Winston

To its dismay, the RGS found that most of the delegates at East St. Louis had never heard of them. Their leader Chino had been elected interim president of YOU at the New York conference; at East St. Louis, Warren Gilmore was elected national president. Racial emphasis on the side of blacks was felt everywhere, if not uttered in formal resolutions. At the end of the conference, YOU had become officially organized, but RGS was little more than a member group. It turned back to its own affairs.

Membership in YOU helped the Conservative Vice Lords in obtaining financing for their programs. So did the Chicago riots in the summer following the assassination of Martin Luther King, Jr., reminding the authorities as they did that *someone* had to keep the ghettos cool. In 1968 and 1969, the Conservative Vice Lords established a number of programs:

> With funds from Sears Roebuck and an alderman who had helped them . . . they opened a small, air-conditioned ice cream parlor in a gutted storefront.
>
> To encourage pride in black history, they opened The African Lion, which featured African clothing and accessories. . .
>
> With a loan from The American National Bank, they opened two Tastee Freez ice cream franchises, hoping to earn money to sustain their non-income-producing programs. The loan, however, proved enough only to cover initial expenses, and both franchises folded.

The Vice Lords on a Chicago street corner.
The Vice Lords by R. Lincoln Keiser, Holt, Rinehart and Winston

Teen Town—a restaurant the Chicago Vice Lords opened with government funds. The *Vice Lords* by R. Lincoln Keiser, Holt, Rhinehart and Winston.

With financial help from Sammy Davis, Jr., they embarked upon Simone, a black cosmetics enterprise. The company did not progress beyond manufacturing sample products, and the Lords consider it their greatest failure.

With four other groups, the Lords formed an economic coalition and with money provided by the First National Bank of Chicago and expertise provided by the Container Corporation of America the coalition formed the West Side Paper Stock Company.

With funding from the Coalition for Youth Action of the U.S. Department of Labor, 20 young Lords and Ladies underwent a 20 week management training program to prepare them to direct Conservative Vice Lord programs.

A street academy for high school drop-outs was opened, and by cooperative arrangement with Malcolm X Community College, continuing education was made possible.

In 1968 the Ford Foundation gave $130,000 to improve the executive skills of Vice Lords leaders. Consultants were paid to be partner-directors to Vice Lord directors of various enterprises. But the grant was for only one year and this was not enough time to define new roles, develop new programs, and at the same time hold the street together.

Beautification and tenants' action programs, art and recreational projects, work with other self-help programs, many other programs were initiated by the Conservative Vice Lords and their allies. Some succeeded, some failed; nearly all depended upon financing from outside sources, private or federal.[45]

During this time, RGS was not idle, but it suffered a series of setbacks. A group of younger Puerto Rican members from East Harlem established a branch of the University of the Streets in El Barrio uptown. Before long the uptown and downtown branches of the University were vying with each other for federal and foundation monies. In the end, the University staff, tired of the infighting in RGS, decided to separate from RGS and get its own funding. But once disconnected from the famous gang image, the University lost much of its grant-getting power. The RGS, after losing the University of the Streets, became torn by even more infighting, and there seemed little likelihood that the Real Great Society would again become a major force for constructive change.

Meanwhile, YOU waited impatiently for its expected grant from OEO, for it could not embark on any real programs without it. The YOU leaders were very optimistic that they would receive the grant, but in June of 1968 their optimism was shattered. About a year earlier the OEO had made a grant of $927,341 for a training and employment program with two Chicago gangs, the Blackstone Rangers and the East Side Disciples. In June, 1968, the OEO was accused by Senator John L. McClellan of Arkansas of supporting street gang activities alleged to include intimidation, fraud, and other criminal behavior. Suddenly, the OEO became cautious, and word went out that no grants would be made until the controversy was cleared

[45] Dawley, pp. 138–146.

up. For 24 months, YOU hobbled along on small, private dona-
tions. Finally, in June 1970, the Nixon Administration was persuaded to make a first year grant of $393,414 for a program
similar to that proposed to OEO.

In 1970, Richard Poston wrote:

> Today's gang leaders have become expert at taking the
> practical art of hustling, expanding its scale, and using it
> on government agencies, foundations, and business firms
> to promote the grants so important to their continued op-
> erations and power. No modern, professional grantsman is
> their superior; the gang leaders obtain professional grants-
> men to write their proposals, then add their own special
> touch to the hustle. Sweet talk, patriotic talk, inspirational
> talk, abrasive talk, blustering talk, demanding talk, intimi-
> dating talk, misleading talk—whatever kind of talk it takes,
> depending on the listener and the situation—the gang lead-
> ers know all the words and how to use them. When to keep
> peace, when to make a show of strength, when to be threat-
> ening—whatever seems to work best at any given moment
> is brought into play. . . From their numerous allies, and
> from their own experience, the gang leaders have learned
> what makes the establishment listen, and have become
> practiced in the art of supplying it.[46]

By 1971 the orgy of proposal-making and grant-making and
money flowing was over. The Nixon Administration announced
drastic cut-backs in social action programs; the Great Society of
Lyndon Johnson was considered a glorious failure. The phenomenon of government-funded programs operated by urban
youth gangs had never really succeeded. Far more numerous
than any actual programs had been all those words, all that
talk, all those myths. The gang leaders, once filled with an idealistic desire to help their communities, had already become a
part of the establishment they wanted to reject, had taken on a

[46] Poston, pp. 252–253.

Mobilization for Youth—one of the youth services programs struggling to survive despite the cutbacks in funding.   *Robert Goldberg*

grant-dependent mentality, had become captives of Washington politics, had looked at money in terms of how much they could direct into their own pockets rather than into the community. They had grown older—too old to be identity models for young ghetto dwellers. They had lost touch with the communities which they had originally wanted to serve.

Even before the Nixon Administration's belt tightening in the area of social action, the establishment-gangs had ceased to enjoy any real influence in the ghettos. Groups like RGS hadn't accomplished much—at least the revolutionary gangs had, in showing their contempt for the system, given ghetto dwellers some satisfaction at seeing the discomfort of the system. Now, even calls for revolution had lost their attraction. The young political confrontation groups began to recast themselves into street gangs.

They did not like to be called "gangs," but referred to themselves as "cliques" in New York and "corners" in Philadelphia. They did not show much interest in rumbles over "turf" or girls, nor were they very interested in violence for its own sake. They engaged in violence for a very specific purpose, to "get" the pushers. Independently, different gangs mounted a campaign of killing and beating against the pushers that showed early signs of reducing the ghetto drug traffic considerably. Some clever pushers, however, managed to take advantage of this campaign for their own ends, hiring gangs to kill rival pushers. The rash of violence made authorities suddenly aware of the existence of the new gangs, and quickly youth workers stepped in, hoping to defuse an explosive situation.

In some cases the gangs themselves took steps to make sure that their violence would not be directed against each other. In the South Bronx, New York, the presidents of the Royal Javelins and the Peacemakers asked a youth worker to help them form a coalition known as the Brotherhood. Their reasons for wanting the coalition: whitey would like nothing better than to see them kill each other off; gang fights only hurt them, not whitey.

A Turban leader (center) takes the floor at a meeting of the Brotherhood.
New York Daily News

By early 1971 the Royal Javelins and the Peacemakers had been joined by the Young Sinners, the Reapers, and the Black Spades. Youth workers helped to initiate other such peace treaties, as did other gang leaders, but the cards were stacked against them. Everyday, ghetto grievances were much more real than any shaky peace treaty. You might know, intellectually, that society wants you to kill each other, but when another gang member looks at your girl or beats on your buddy, you forget about society and settle your score. Not a few would-be truce makers were killed for their efforts.

There was another reason why an anti-drug alliance such as the Brotherhood would have trouble surviving. The major dealers who supplied the South Bronx were determined that nothing should interfere with their business. Like the corrupt politicians and factory owners of earlier times, the pushers hired gangs to do their dirty work. Armed by the dealers, willing gangs were paid to destroy other gangs who had declared themselves against drugs.

In early 1972 the gangs were making headlines again. Reports of street gang activity in New York, Philadelphia and Los Angeles showed a reversal of the statistics of a few years before. Now, drug use seemed to be decreasing and, correspondingly, gang violence was increasing. Only Chicago, did not conform to the pattern. They were still into drugs, but the Chicago gangs had not succumbed to drugs as early as the gangs of New York and Los Angeles. As a former Chicago "gang-banger" explained:

> More brothers getting killed because there are more guns. But gang-bangin' itself is dying off. Now, too many brothers are too busy noddin' on the junk.[47]

As the latest rash of gang activities was occurring, the newspapers were busy guessing just how the latest gang era would develop. Amid the ifs and the possibilities were certain definite facts. (1) Gang membership was growing, ranging from 4,000 to 6,000 in each of the four cities. (2) Gang-related violence was on the increase. In the Bronx, New York, in 1972, gangs were blamed by police for 30 murders, 22 attempted homicides, 300 assaults, 10 rapes and 124 armed robberies, resulting in some 1,500 gang arrests. In 1962, there were only 12 youth gang homicides reported in the entire city. In the first six months of 1973, 27 gang-related murders were reported in New York and 16 in Los Angeles. (3) The potential for violence was far greater for the gangs had access to weapons that no gang had ever had before.

The gangs of today are similar in many ways to the gangs of the past, and in many ways they are different. Like gangs before they are usually formed by young ghetto dwellers for protection, for some sense of belonging in a world where there is often little home life and little positive sense of identity, for a

[47] Donald Jackson, "Youth Gangs' Violence Found Rising in 3 Cities," *New York Times* (April 16, 1972), p. 58.

Two girl members display their gang's colors.   *Steve Salmieri*

variety of very human, very understandable reasons. In Chicago,
a Black Disciple explains it this way:

> Gangs give folks something to be proud of. My parents
> couldn't afford to put me in the Boy Scouts. So me and the
> rest of our guys started getting together. Our main func-
> tion is to help a brother. It's a thing where guys care about
> each other.[48]

They get together, and to show that they are together, to
give their *group* some identity, they choose names to inspire
fear and respect, names like: Savage Skulls, Black Assassins,
Savage Nomads, Majestic Warlocks, Brothers of Satan, Reapers,
Henchmen, Black Spades, Dirty Dozen.

Each gang also has its own "colors" or insignia, which is
worn on the back of their jackets. Although these "colors" usu-

[48] *Times* (April 16, 1972), p. 58.

ally feature skulls, flames, the devil, some are different; one gang's "colors" are a top hat, cane and white gloves on a red and green background. In the 1940's and 1950's, the jackets were usually of leather, but now they tend to be dungaree jackets. Perhaps this was in imitation of the Hell's Angels, although many young people wear such jackets today. In fact, gang members follow the latest trends in young people's fashions, wearing army surplus clothing, and distinctive hats. A few gangs do not wear jackets with "colors" and choose other distinctive uniforms. The Crips, a rapidly growing gang in Los Angeles, prefer a black glove, on the left hand, a gold earring for the left ear lobe, and a cane. According to gang legend, the name and the cane derive from the fact that the gang's founders were crippled when they started the gang and used walking sticks.

While the earliest organized gangs made their headquarters in greengrocery stores and the gangs of the 1940's and 1950's frequented neighborhood candy stores, today's gangs generally prefer more private headquarters. Although the majority of gang members technically live at home, they spend as little time at home as possible; some gang members are estranged from their families and really have no home. To both groups, real "home" is headquarters—a tenement basement or apartment, heated by a gas oven, paint chipping off the walls, often without hot water. Such headquarters represent a real haven from the dangerous streets and from the hatred of society, as well as a place to get a good night's sleep.

Some gangs find apartments in abandoned buildings for their headquarters, although they know they will eventually have to move when the building is torn down. Some gangs pay the rent on apartments in occupied buildings by charging members' dues. Others use more ingenious methods. The Royal Javelins in the Bronx "persuaded" a frightened building superintendent to give them the use of a three-room basement apartment in return for their protecting the tenants and keeping the building clean. Although both landlord and tenants had grave misgivings about the arrangement at first, after awhile they relaxed and, in some cases, were actually pleased. The tenants indeed felt safer, and the gang also kept its promise to keep the building clean.

The gangs' headquarters are similar in appearance. As they are so often the sleeping quarters of the members, they are furnished chiefly with couches wedged tightly against one another and with mattresses strewn helter-skelter on the floor. The walls are covered with day-glo paintings of the gangs' "colors," slogans, members' names and nicknames, and often these paintings are illuminated by fluorescent lights.

Some gangs, however, reject the whole idea of a stable, lasting headquarters. Another Bronx gang, the Reapers, would never have one:

> "You'll never catch me in a clubhouse, brother," said one young Reaper, nodding toward a passing police car. "There, the Man knows where you are, and he can come down on you whenever he wants." He pulled a six-inch blade from the pocket of his denim jacket and said, "Sometimes you just can't afford to get popped in on, know what I mean?" [49]

Courage and fighting ability have traditionally been the qualities most respected by the gangs, and today gang leaders must be courageous and good fighters in order to retain their positions. Gang leaders today, however, must also have intelligence. Ask a gang member about his leader and he will almost invariably smile knowingly, tap his forehead, and say. "It's what's up here that counts." Almost every gang leader is extremely articulate and a "good administrator,"—good at delegating authority, good at getting things done, good at getting others to follow him. It is natural, among today's street gangs, that intelligence is so respected. Formerly, courage and fighting ability were all important because winning gang fights and being successful in other gang activities depended chiefly upon phys-

---

[49] Gene Weingarten, "East Bronx Story—Return of the Street Gangs," *New York Magazine* (March 27, 1972), p. 36.

An armed gang member.   *James Haskins*

ical strength and skill. By the 1950's, guns had begun to replace the brass knuckles and chains and iron pipes and naked fists, and by the 1960's and 1970's, as the Black Panthers had so aptly put it, "guns were key." If a cat had a gun, he didn't need physical strength or courage, but he did need intelligence, because everyone else had a gun, too, not just crude zip-guns, but homemade bazookas and factory-made pieces. In 1972 a magazine reporter wrote:

> Today there is scarcely a gang in the Bronx that cannot muster a factory-made piece for every member—at the very least a .22 caliber pistol, but quite often heavier stuff: .32s, .38s, and .45s, shotguns, rifles, and—I have seen them myself—even machine guns, grenades, and gelignite, an explosive. One gang, the Royal Javelins, has acquired some walkie-talkie radios.[50]

Many magazine and newspaper reporters theorized that organized crime, black and white, had gotten the youth gangs interested in sophisticated weapons. When the authorities started becoming aware of renewed gang activity, the newspapers and magazines picked up the story. When reports that the youth gangs were back hit the papers and magazines, the reporters suggested, munitions salesmen dispatched by the underworld made their way to the areas of reported gang activity to announce their readiness to deal in hand guns, explosives, machine guns and grenades. "Earlier this month," a reporter wrote in March of 1973, "a large clique in the Northern Bronx concluded a deal—one of the gang insists it was with the Black Panthers—for four high-powered rifles and 'several' .38 revolvers. Reported price: just under $300."[51]

Certainly, a potential new market like the rising number of street gangs would be eagerly taken advantage of by underworld munitions salesmen, but it would be unrealistic to suggest

[50] Ibid., p. 34.
[51] Ibid.

that they force or influence the gangs to purchase weapons from them. As the 1950's gang member said, "If a gang wants pieces, it gets pieces."

Television and the new "urban action" movies have introduced the youngest gang member to the range of sophisticated weaponry. Knowing that such weapons exist, few are going to opt for old-style fighting tools.

The chief reason for acquiring manufactured guns and other modern weapons is, of course, protection. Just as, in the late 40's and early 50's, the presence on the block of one youth with a gun, whether he could shoot straight or not, prompted others to get guns, the possession of factory-made guns by a 1970's gang makes it necessary for other gangs to acquire such guns. It is a ghetto arms race, and just like arms races between nations, it is potentially very dangerous. It is too easy for the power of arms to be abused, and already the tragic results of the gangs' weapons build-up are evident in the increased numbers of killings and injuries.

Today's gangs, in addition to having much more sophisticated weapons, also have much greater legal and political so-

Graffitti and the names of local gangs decorate a playground wall.
Robert Goldberg

phistication. Often, the gang leader is responsible for the safety of the gang, which is another reason why intelligence has come to be a very respected quality among the gangs. For example, the tendency of gang members to have nicknames has a very serious purpose behind it. Police jot down names they hear on the street and compile files on these names. To help make these files less meaningful and less dangerous, almost every gang member takes a nickname when he joins the gang. From then on, he is known only by that nickname, and often his fellow gang members do not know his real name.

When it becomes apparent to a gang that someone must be arrested for a crime, often the gang itself chooses that "someone." Usually a minor is chosen, because his prison sentence is likely to be shorter. And the minor agrees because serving a term in jail helps to boost his "rep."

Further proof of the gangs' knowledge of the law, particularly laws which protect citizens against injustice on the part of legal authorities, is shown in the following incident:

> . . . 14 members of the Dirty Dozen . . . were arrested, apparently on their way to a rumble. The police say the gang members immediately threw to the ground a loaded sawed-off shotgun, a loaded .32 and assorted knives and chains. One member was held for parole violation, and the rest were released on their own recognizance.
>
> Judge Dennis Edwards Jr. of the Bronx Criminal Court remembers the case vaguely as "an adjournment in contemplation of dismissal." The police acknowledge that there was no way of proving who was carrying what weapons, or that the weapons were even in the possession of the youths.
>
> "They found the guns on the ground and tried to blame us," protests Slick, a member of the Dirty Dozen. It was his eighth arrest with no convictions. Slick is 15 years old.[52]

[52] *Times* (January 16, 1973), p. 28.

Members of the Spanish Kings patrolling their territory.

New York Daily News

In studying the law to learn how it can protect them, the gangs are following the lead of the Black Panthers and other groups that arose in the late 1960's. The Panthers, in their early days, used to walk through the streets carrying guns and "patroling the police" to guard against police harassment of ghetto residents. Having studied the gun laws, they knew they had a right to carry guns as long as they were not concealed. Naturally, the police frequently stopped them, and as passers-by looked on, the Panthers would remind the police that they had a perfect right to carry guns and, what's more, if the police shot at them, they had a right to shoot back in self-defense. By this time a crowd had usually gathered, but when the police tried to disperse them the Panthers would quote the law that crowds may remain to watch an incident as long as they are "a reasonable distance" away.

With the greater sophistication and greater access to guns of today's gangs, some officials at first did not expect that the tradition of rumbles would be carried on. But recent newspaper reports show that the rumbles are returning as the gangs continue to increase and start to crowd one another. The concept of turf—of territoriality—has always been basic to the existence of a gang. A 1950's gang member put it this way:

> We needed land to establish our identity and we really didn't own land. But we thought this was ours and we paraded the streets and occupied certain corners.[53]

Now, as the ghettos become more and more overcrowded, a gang's territory may be no more than a single corner or a block at best, and it is essential to protect that territory. But the rumbles of today are not the mass melees of years past. Nor are they hours long, as they used to be. Guns are responsible. Guns decide arguments very quickly and are much more deadly than fists or chains or lead pipes. Gang wars today are usually fought like guerrilla warfare, with sniping from rooftops and quick shots from speeding cars replacing face to face confrontations. They are also much more difficult for the police to anticipate and stop than the old-style, large-scale rumbles.

Like all gangs in history, the gangs of today like publicity. It is in this area that their legal sophistication does not hold, for publicity is always potentially harmful for a gang. Like the gang members that Jacob Riis found to photograph, gang members of today who pose for photographers are eager to do so. They display their colors, try to look as suave or as tough as possible,

[53] Dawley, p. 25.

The Seven Immortals in their headquarters.   Steve Salmieri

or strike comical poses. None, for obvious reasons, will consent to be photographed holding a piece, but those members of gangs who have walkie-talkies will pose with such electronic wonders.

Although their legal sophistication dissolves when it comes to publicity, the gangs' political sophistication holds true. Gang members can appear on television and be remarkably poised, and many a viewer finds himself thinking, "Gee, they're really good kids, they just haven't had a chance." They can be interviewed by newspaper and magazine reporters and make sure their feelings are communicated.

What the gangs of today stress most to the publicity-givers are their non-criminal goals: eviction of pushers from their neighborhoods, clean-up of streets and back lots, registration of voters, and even peace among gangs. They ban drugs, they insist, and live by strict codes of behavior. The rules of the Seven Immortals in the Bronx are illustrative:

1. No playing with hands. (No gestures while talking.)
2. No giving cigarettes to young or baby Immortals.
3. No drinking before meeting.
4. No looking for trouble.
5. No writing names in hallways, fences, walls, windows.
6. No wearing colors on Sundays, unless specified.
7. Colors will be respected.
8. Earrings—crosses only, left ear only.
9. Immortal girls will be respected.
10. Heads [addicts] will be respected.
11. All meetings must be attended, unless specified.
12. Colors must be flown on our own turf.

ANYONE DISOBEYING THIS ORDER WILL GET SEVEN LASHES FROM EACH MEMBER.[54]

There are other rules the gangs prefer not to mention. One such rule prohibits a gang member from quitting the gang. Ac-

[54] *Times* (January 16, 1973), p. 28.

cording to New York City police, many of the 30 gang-attributed homicides that occurred in the city in 1972 were killings of gang members who wanted to quit their gangs. So were many of the assaults and attempted homicides. One girl attempted to leave the "ladies" auxiliary of the Seven Immortals. She was subjected to the punishment decreed for breaking one of the twelve rules posted by the Immortals—only more severe. She was made to run between two lines of gang members, who beat her with chains and belts. The beating was so severe that the girl was crippled for life.

Today's gangs also commit their share of crimes "just for kicks." Although they often insist they want good relations with the community, sometimes they engage in senseless acts of violence against innocent passers-by, and there is evidence that such "just for kicks" violence will increase. When you get down to basics, the conditions that have fertilized the soil for gang violence throughout American history exist, essentially unchanged, today. The human needs of the new street gangs are no different from the gangs of the past, the difference is that today's gang members are more politically aware and their potential for violence is much greater.

With sophisticated weapons comes a sense of power much more immediate and real than any budding sense of political power that might have once touched the new street gang's consciousness. After all, what *can* they do against the system compared to what they can do against each other and against the other hapless inhabitants of the ghetto? And it *is* a sense of power they seek most, or rather an escape from a sense of powerlessness. No one wants to be "nobody," no one wants to be poor; no one wants to live forever amid the hopelessness of the ghetto. As long as these conditions exist, the street gang will continue to exist. Herbert Asbury and Jacob Riis pointed out this truth nearly three-quarters of a century ago; yet it is sadly necessary to point it out once again.

BIBLIOGRAPHY

Allen, Robert L. *Black Awakening in Capitalist America: An Analytic History.* Garden City, N.Y.: Doubleday, 1969.

Asbury, Herbert. *The Gangs of New York: An Informal History of the Underworld.* New York: Alfred A. Knopf, 1927.

Bernstein, Saul. *Youth on the Streets: Work with Alienated Youth Gangs.* New York: Association Press, 1964.

Cartwright, Dorwin, and Alvin Zander, eds. *Group Dynamics: Research and Theory,* 2nd edition. New York: Harper and Row, 1960.

Clark, Kenneth B. *Dark Ghetto: Dilemmas of Social Power.* New York: Harper and Row, 1965.

Cordasco, Francisco, ed. *Jacob Riis Revisited: Poverty and the Slum in Another Era.* Garden City, N.Y.: Doubleday, 1968.

Crawford, Paul L., et al. *Working with Teen-Age Gangs.* New York: Welfare Council of New York, 1950.

Dawley, David. *A Nation of Lords: The Autobiography of the Vice Lords.* Garden City, N.Y.: Doubleday, 1973.

Ellis, Edward Robb. *The Epic of New York City.* New York: Coward-McCann, Inc., 1966.

Gage, Nicholas. "The Mafia at War," Part I. *New York Magazine,* July 10, 1972, pp. 30–44.

———. "The Mafia at War," Part II. *New York Magazine,* July 17, 1972, pp. 27–36.

Gibbens, T. C. N., and R. H. Ahrenfeldt, eds. *Cultural Factors in Delinquency.* Philadelphia: J.B. Lippincott Co., 1966.

Handlin, Oscar. *The Newcomers: Negroes and Puerto Ricans in a Changing Metropolis.* Garden City, N.Y.: Doubleday, 1962.

Handlin, Oscar, and Mary F. Handlin. *Facing Life: Youth and the Family in American History.* Boston: Little, Brown & Co., 1971.

Hanson, Kitty. "Teeners Run Wild in Theft, Dope, Sex," New York *Daily News,* August 21, 1962, pp. 34+.

————. "Youth Board Helps—Some," New York *Daily News,* August 23, 1962, pp. 3+.

Haskins, James. *Profiles in Black Power.* Garden City, N.Y.: Doubleday, 1972.

Janson, Donald. "Youth Gangs' Violence Found Rising in 3 Cities," *New York Times,* April 16, 1972, pp. 1+.

"Mass Murder Trial," *Life,* March 17, 1958, pp. 30–31.

"Massacre in New York," *Newsweek,* September 7, 1959, pp. 32–33.

Morrison, Christopher. "Could This Happen to Your Boy?" *Look,* November 2, 1954, pp. 124–129.

Nevins, Allan, ed. *The Diary of Philip Hone.* New York: Dodd, Mead, 1936.

New York City Youth Board. *Reaching the Fighting Gang.* New York: New York City Youth Board, 1960.

Osofsky, Gilbert. *Harlem: The Making of a Ghetto.* New York: Harper and Row, 1968.

"Peacemaking Priest in Gangland," *Life,* August 26, 1957, pp. 89–92.

Pileggi, Nicholas. "The Mafia: Serving Your Community Since 1890," *New York Magazine,* July 24, 1972, pp. 39–51.

Poston, Richard W. *The Gang and the Establishment.* New York: Harper and Row, 1971.

Rand, Christopher. *The Puerto Ricans.* New York: Oxford University Press, 1958.

Randel, William Peirce. *The Ku Klux Klan: A Century of Infamy.* Philadelphia: Chilton Books, 1965.

Rice, Robert. "Six Nights with a Teenage Gang," *New York Post,* June 4, 1958, pp. M1, 2.

Riis, Jacob. *How the Other Half Lives.* New York: Dover Publishers, 1971.

Sanders, Wiley B. *Juvenile Offenders of 1000 Years.* University of North Carolina Press, 1970.

Short, James F. Jr., ed. *Gang Delinquency and Delinquent Subcultures.* New York: Harper and Row, 1968.

Spergel, Irving. *Racketville, Slumtown, Haulberg: An Exploratory Study of Delinquent Subcultures.* Chicago: University of Chicago Press, 1964.

Stokes, I. N. Phelps. *The Iconography of Manhattan,* (6 Vols.) Vol. V., New York: Robert H. Dodd, 1915.

"Teen-Age Terror on the New York Streets," *Life,* July 11, 1955, pp. 33–35.

Thompson, Hunter S. *Hell's Angels: A Strange and Terrible Saga.* New York: Random House, 1966.

Tolchin, Martin. "Gangs Spread Terror in the South Bronx," *New York Times,* January 16, 1973, pp. 1+.

_____. "South Bronx: A Jungle Stalked by Fear, Seized by Rage," *New York Times,* January 15, 1973, pp. 1+.

Wakefield, Dan. *Island in the City: The World of Spanish Harlem.* Boston: Houghton Mifflin, 1957.

Weingarten, Gene. "East Bronx Story—Return of the Street Gangs," *New York Magazine,* March 27, 1972, pp. 31–37.

ACKNOWLEDGEMENTS

Grateful thanks are due to Ruth Ann Stewart for helping with the researching of this book, to Susan Kalhoefer for typing the manuscript, and to Kathy Benson, whose help proved indispensable.

GLOSSARY

Slang changes from month to month and block to block, but here are some striking expressions used by gang members in the nineteenth and early twentieth centuries, and in the decades following World War II.

SLANG OF EARLY GANGS

Anointed—Flogged
Balsam—Money
Baptized—Liquor that has been watered
Barking irons—Pistols
Ben—A rest
Benjamin—A coat
Bens—Fools
Bingo—Liquor
Black-box—A lawyer
Bleak—Handsome, pretty
Bleak mort—A pretty girl
Bloke—A man
Blunt—Money
Booly dog—A policeman
Brads—Money
Brass—Money

Buzz—To search for and steal
Can—A dollar
Canary bird—A convict
Caravan—Plenty of money
Casa—A house
Case—A dollar
Cat—A prostitute;
    a cross old woman
Century—One hundred dollars
Chink—Money
Chips—Money
City College—The Tombs prison
Cove or covey—A man
Cows and kisses—The ladies
Crib—A house
Crusher—A policeman
Cull—A man; sometimes a partner
Dace—Two cents
Daddles—Hands
Dangler—A seducer
Devil books—Cards
Dews—Ten dollars
Diddle—Liquor
Diddle cove—A landlord
Dimber mort—A pretty girl
Dots—Money
Eriffs—Young thieves
Evil—A wife
Fanny Blair—The hair
Fenced—Sold
Finniff—Five dollars
Fork—A pickpocket
Frog—A policeman
Gagers—Eyes
Gan—The mouth or lips
Gelter—Money
Gip—A thief
Gooseberry pudding—A woman
Ground sweat—A grave
Gun—A thief
Harp—A woman

Hockey—Drunk
Hogg—A ten cent piece
Hoister—A shoplifter
Jack—A small coin; money
Jaw coves—Lawyers
Kiddies—Young thieves
Kitchen physic—Food
Lib—Sleep
Marking—Observing
Moll—A woman
Moon—One month
Mort—A woman
Mow—To kiss
Much—Money
My Uncle—A pawnbroker
Nose—A spy, an informer
Ochre—Money
Ogles—The eyes
O.K.—All right
Pad—A street; a highway
Pad the hoof—Walk the street
Pig—A policeman
Pigeon—An informer
Pop—To pawn
Pops—Pistols
Popshop—Pawnbroker's shop
Rabbit—A rowdy. "Dead Rabbit," a very athletic, rowdy fellow
Rag—A dollar
Reader—A pocketbook
Regulars—Share or portion
Rhino—Money
Rub us to whit—Send us to prison
Sam—A stupid fellow
Sawney—Bacon; fat pork
Shakester—A lady
Stretch—One year
Vamp—To pledge
Velvet—The tongue
Venus' curse—Venereal disease
Whit—A prison
Yam—To eat

SLANG OF MODERN GANGS

Apple—Money

Bad—Good

Bad mouth—To talk about someone maliciously

Bat—Woman

Bear—Woman

Blood—Friend; a black; money

Blow change—To think, talk, write or play music along the lines of revolutionary principles

Bomb—Deception

Bopping—Fighting

Bread—Money

Brother—Friend

Bug—To annoy, irritate

Bulls—Police

Burn—Kill

Busted—Arrested

Cake—Money

Cat—Man

Chick—Woman

Cool—A peaceful condition between groups

Cool it—Be calm

Crazy—A term of endearment; shrewd; having a special way of looking at things

Cut-out—Leave the scene rapidly

Deal—Woman

Debs—Girls' auxiliary of a gang

Deck—A standard package of mixed heroin

Did a nickel—Served five months in prison

Ditty bop—Variation on bopping, usually the activity of younger gang members

Down kiddies—Skilled street fighters in a rumble

Dozens—A verbal assault on the parent, especially the mother of another

Dude—Man

Dumb—Clever

Dust—Money

Falling out—To arrive at a party looking sharp
Fish—Woman
Five calendars—Five months
Fox—Woman
Give some skin—Shake hands
Groovy—Excellent, enjoyable
Hangout—Meeting place for a gang
Happy shop—Liquor store
Hawk—To walk rapidly
Heart—Qualities of courage, etc. in confronting rival gangs
Hep—Understand
Hip—Understand
Hooked—Dependent upon narcotics and unable to quit
Hustle—To survive by any means possible
Hype—Deception
Ice—Ignore
Jack—Money
Jam—To party; make exciting music
Jazz—Music; cluttered conversation used to confuse
Jim—Man
Jive stud—A braggart, liar and status seeker
Junky—One who is hooked on drugs
Laid in the aisle—Well dressed, stylish
Let it all hang out—Be uninhibited, free
Lightup Man—Street gang member whose job is doing the shooting;
    the key person of an advance party
Man, the—Those in power; police
Nod—Hair; stupor-like state brought on by drugs
Numbers—Illegal gambling on a series of three numbers
O.K.—Correct, right
Out to lunch—In a state in which one does not want to or cannot
    understand
Packing—Armed with a concealed weapon
Pad—Home, place to stay
Piece—Gun
Pigs—Police
Pull your coattail—Make you aware
Punked out—Ceased activity, finked out
Raise—To get out of jail
Rap—To tell the truth; to talk
Rep—Reputation, face, status

Right on—Tell the truth; say what must be said

Rip off—To steal

Rod—Gun

Rumble—Armed conflict between two or more rival street gangs

Run down—Keep talking; hurry and tell me

Short—Automobile

Sneaky Pete—Inexpensive wine

Sounding—Verbal attack on the club or its members

Squeeze—Girlfriend; boyfriend; intimate acquaintance

Stoned—Intoxicated by narcotics or alcohol

Stumpers—Shoes

Sweat box—Crowded party

Trap—Military draft board

Turn out—To break up

Waste—To destroy the opposition; exhaustion as a result of participation in a conflict

Wild—Deeply satisfying

Wild kiddies—Provocative gang members who start conflicts with
no sense of control or concern for consequences

INDEX

Gangs denoted by g, leaders or members by gl or gm

Ah Ken, 58
American Daily Advertiser, 19
American Guards g, 28
American National Bank, 118
American Revolution, 17, 18, 19
Apprentices, 14-16, 19, 20, 21
Army, U.S., 29, 40
Asbury, Herbert, 33, 51, 56, 64, 78
Astor Foundation, 112, 113
Atlantic Guards g, 28, 36

El Barrio, 82, 121
Big Jack Zelig (William Alberts), 63, 64
Black Muslims. 109
Black Panthers, 109, 131, 134, 135
Blacks, 79, 80, 81, 82, 86, 96, 117, 118; civil rights movement, 107; killed in Draft Riot, 39, 40; and Ku Klux Klan, 44, 45; migrate from South, 68; from West Indies, 78
Blackstone Rangers g, 121
Bootlegging, 68, 71, 72, 76
Border Gang g, 33
Boston, Mass., 18
Bowery, the (N.Y.C.), 27, 28, 32, 34

Bowery Boys g, 27, 28
Bow Kum, 60, 61
Brando, Marlon, 91, 92
Bronx (N.Y.C.), 96, 126, 129, 131, 133
Brooklyn, N.Y., 69, 71, 73, 82, 96
Brotherhood g, 124, 125

Capo di tutti capi, 73
Capone, Al gl, 69, 71, 72
Camorra, 69-71
Carson, Wild Maggie gl, 56
Charleston Street Gang, 34
Chicago, Ill., 69, 71, 72, 76, 80, 81, 107, 116, 119, 126
Chichesters g, 27, 41
Child Labor Law, 53
Chinatown (N.Y.C.), 58-61
Chinese, 58-61
Civil Rights Movement, 107
Civil War, 37, 41
Cleaver, Eldridge, 109
"Cliques," 87, 124
Coalition for Youth Action, (CYA), 116, 120
Cocaine, 51
Coleman, Edward gl, 25, 26
Colombo, Joseph, 74, 75

Colonization of America, 14
Colored Orphan Asylum, 40
Commissione, 73
Conscription Act 1863, 37, 38
Conservatives, The g, 103, 104
Conservative Vice Lords g, 116, 118-121
Consiglieri, 73
Container Corp. of America, 120
"corners," 124
Count Benny gl, 86
CYA, *See* Coalition for Youth Action

Dagger Debs g, 97
Dago Frank (Cirofici, Frank) gm, 63
Davis, Sammy Jr., 120
Daybreak Boys g, 33, 34, 56
Dead Rabbits g, 27-29, 31, 33, 36, 37, 50
Depression, the, 78, 79, 81
Detroit, Mich., 107
Diaz, Victor gl, 88
Dirty Dozen g, 133
Dopey Benny gl, 66
Draft Riots, the, 37-41
Dragons g, 87, 88
Drug pushers, 107; exploitation of gangs by, 125, 126; gang war on, 124
Drug use, 50, 51, 100, 104, 105, 107, 124, 126
Dutch Heinrichs gl, 47

East Harlem (N.Y.C.), 82, 86, 87, 109, 121
East River (N.Y.C.), 34, 89
East St. Louis Mo., 117, 188
East Side (N.Y.C.), 81, 84, 96, 107, 110, 111, 115
East Side Disciples g, 121
Eastman, Monk (Osterman) gl, 58, 63
Eastmans g, 43, 57, 58
East Village (N.Y.C.), 114
Edwards, Judge Dennis Jr., 133
Eighteenth Amendment, *See* Prohibition, Volstead Act, 68, 69
Enchanters, The g, 86, 87, 102, 103

Ethnic groups, 82, 117, *See* Gangs, ethnic composition, *See also* Chinese, Germans, Irish, etc.

"Fence," definition of, 41
First National Bank of Chicago, 120
Five Pointers g, 43, 57, 58
Five Points, the (N.Y.C.), 24-27, 31, 32, 36, 42
Ford Foundation, 120
Forty Thieves g, 26, 27
Four Brothers (tong), 60

Gangs: battles between, 28, 29, 57-58, 61-62, 66, 135; "bopping," 85, 86, 96; business ventures of, 112, 119-121; California, 92; Chinese, 58-61; coalitions of, 124; "colors" of, 127, 128; community action of, 109, 110, 112, 115, 116, 120, 121, 122-124, 128; crime statistics on, 126; definition of, 13, 77; drug use by, 50, 51, 100, 105, 124, 126; ethnic composition of, 22, 47, 58, 71, 77, 82, 86, 87; female, 96, 97, 139; first in N.Y.C., 26; German, 47, 58; "going social," 102, 104; grant seeking by, 11, 112, 116, 120-122; headquarters, *See* Headquarters; "honor of," 36, 37; Irish, 27, 30, 39, 63, 71, 82; Italian, 47, 63, 69-71, 74, 77, 82, 86, 87; Jewish, 62, 71, 89; "jitterbugging," 96; juvenile, 53, 56, 78, 96, 97; labor disputes, use in, 66, 67; leaders of, *See* Gang leaders; legal sophistication of, 132, 133, 134, 135; literature about, 100; media influence on, 48, 90, 92-94, 132, 135, 136; members, *See* Gang members; motorcycle, 91-93; movie influence on, 90; names of, 43, 47, 56, 66, 83, 86, 96, 97, 125; Polish, 71; politicians, use by, 31, 32, 34, 35, 57, 58; publicity seeking by, 48, 49, 74, 90, 135, 136, Puerto Rican, 82, 84, 86, 87, 93, 96, 109, 110, 117; reasons for, 52, 53, 77, 127, 139; reprisal by, 87; riverfront 33, 34; rules of, 101, 138, 139; violent crimes by, 30, 42, 50, 64, 88-90, 139; war on pushers, 124-126; weapons of *See* Weapons

Gang leaders, 13, 26, 42, 62, 64-66, 71-74, 76, 97, 109, 122; qualities of, 129, 133

Gang members: ages of, 31, 33, 77, 133; characteristics of, 77, 78, 94, 95, 101, 102; descriptions of, 31, 48, 50, 53, 122, 126, 127, 129; dress of, 12, 27, 31, 42, 43, 47, 83, 84, 94, 127, 128; female, 29, 55, 56, 139; juvenile, 53, 56, 57, 78, 96, 97; mannerisms of, 85; nicknames of, 33, 63, 133; numbers of, 34, 65, 126; pressures on, 101, 102, 106; search for identity by, 47, 48; weapons of, *See* Weapons

Gas Housers g, 43, 47

Germans, 47, 58

"getting high," 104

Ghetto, 80, 107, 108, 110, 111, 115, 123, 125, 132, 139

Gilmore, Warren, 116-118

"going social," 102, 104

Gophers g, 42, 43, 50, 57, 64, 65

Great Society, The, 111, 112

Greengroceries, 25-27

"growler," 52, 53

Gyp the Blood (Harry Horowitz), g, 63

Harlem (N.Y.C.), 63, 69, 79, 81, history of, 80

Hartley Mob g, 47

Hell-Cat Maggie gm, 29

Hell's Angels g, 92, 93, 128

Hell's Kitchen, 42, 47, 64

Hell's Kitchen Gang g, 47

Heroin, 104, 106, 107

Hip Sing (tong), 59-61

Homeless children, 16, 20-22, 53

Hone, Philip, 25, 51

Headquarters of gangs: 128, 129 beer gardens, 27; candy stores, 86; clubrooms, 47; greengroceries, 25-27

Hot Corn Girls, 24

Howlett, William gm, 33

Hudson Dusters g, 43, 50, 51

Hudson River, 34

Immigration, 14, 22, 24, 25, 68, 69

Irish, the, 22, 24, 25, 27, 31, 39, 62, 63, 82

Italian American Civil Rights League, 75

Italians, the, 47, 62, 63, 69-71, 74, 77, 82, 86, 87

Jamaica, N.Y., 96

Jews, the, 62, 71, 80-82, 89

Joe the Greaser gl, 66

"Junk," 126 *See* drug use

Kelly, Paul (Vacarelli), gl, 58, 63

Kerryonians g, 27

Kim Lan Wui Saw (tong), 61

King, Martin Luther Jr., 118

Knockout drops, 47

Ku Klux Klan, 43-45; origin, 43; goals, 43; rise and fall, 44, 45

Labor Dept. of, 116, 120

Lansky, Meyer gl, 73

Lawndale (area of Chicago, Ill.), 80, 81

Laudanum, 50

Lefty Louis (Louis Rosenberg), gm, 63

Little Rhody gl, 66

Los Angeles, Calif., 107, 117, 126, 127, 128

Low Hee Tong gm, 60, 61

Lower East Side, *See* East Side

Luciano, Lucky gl, 72, 73, 74

Lustig, Billy gl, 66

MacIntosh, Ebenezer, 18

Madden, Owen gl, 64

Mafia: origin, 69-71; Capone era, 71, 72; reorganized by Columbo, 74-75; reorganized by Luciano, 73-74; officer's titles, 73; modernized, 73, 74, 75, 76

Mafiosi, See Mafia

Malcolm X, 109

Malcolm X Community College, 120

Manhattan (N.Y.C.), 69, 96

Marijuana, 104, 106

Market Street Commandos g, 92

Marvin, Lee, 91, 92

McClellan, Sen. John L., 121

Milwaukee, Wisc., 116

Mobs, 17, 18, 19, 37-40

Mock Duck gl, 60

Montgomery Guards g, 48

Montresor, Philip, 16, 17

Mott St. (N.Y.C.), 58

Mulberry Bend (area N.Y.C.), 41, 42

Mulberry, St. (N.Y.C.), 24, 27

National Guard, 29, 35, 36

New Orleans, La., 117

New York Central Railroad, 64

New York City, 16, 20, 22, 24-27, 34, 37-42, 47, 53, 56, 57, 72, 78, 79, 107, 116, 126, *See* also streets and areas marked (N.Y.C.)

New York City Youth Board, 97, philosophy of, 99, 100

New York Times, 36, 38

Newton, Huey, 109

Newark, N.J., 107

Nixon Administration, 122, 123

North River (N.Y.C.), 62

O'Brien, Buck gl, 64

O'Connell Guards g, 28

Office of Economic Opportunity (OEO), 111, 112, 115, 121, 122

Old Brewery, the, 24

Omerta, 70, 71, 75

One Lung Curran gl, 91

On Leong (tong), 59, 60, 61

Orphanages, 14, 21, 40, 53

Orphans, 14, 19, 21

Paradise Square (N.Y.C.), 24, 25, 27, 28

Peacemakers g, 124, 125

Peers, Rosanna, 25-27

Pell St. (N.Y.C.), 58, 60

Philadelphia, Pa., 19, 20, 22, 107, 124

Piker Ryan gm, 42

Pinchey Paul gl, 66

Plug Uglies g, 27, 31, 33

Police, 29, 34-38, 40, 43, 50, 53, 56-58, 60, 61, 64, 65, 66, 67, 97, 98, 109, 126, 129, 133, 134, 139

Police Riots, 37

"Popes Day," 18

Polish, the, 71

Poston, Richard, 115, 122

Prohibition, 68, 69, 71, *See* Eighteenth Amendment, Volstead Act

Puerto Ricans, the, 68, 81, 82, 84, 86, 87, 93, 96, 109, 110, 117

Pulaski, Tennessee, 43, 44, 45

Purroy, John, 66

"Racketeering," 69, 70

Rand, Christopher, 84

Real Great Society (RGS), 111, 112, 114-118, 121, 124

Reconstruction Act 1867, 45

Reform movements, 51, 52, 95, 97-99, 101, 110, 112-124

"rep," 106

RGS, *See* Real Great Society

Riis, Jacob, 48, 50, 52, 53, 56, 60

Riots, 17, 18, 28, 29, 36-40

Rivington St., (N.Y.C.), 57

Rivington Street Battle, the, 57, 58

Rockefeller Foundation, 116

Roach Guards g, 27, 28, 31, 36

Royal Javelins g, 124, 125, 128, 131

Sacramento, Calif., 107, 117

St. Valentines Day Massacre, 72

San Francisco, Calif., 61, 116, 117

Saul, Nicholas gm, 32, 33

Schultz, Dutch gl, 69, 73

Seale, Bobby, 109

Sears Roebuck, 119

Secret societies, 58, 69-71
Seminoles g, 88
Shirt Tails g, 27
Short Tails g, 33
Sirocco, Jack gl, 63
Slums, 24, 46, 51, 56, 90, *See* Ghetto
Smugglers, 17
"Social club", 50, 102, 104
Society for Prevention of Cruelty to Children, 56
Sons of Liberty, 18
South Bronx (N.Y.C.) 124, 125, *See* Bronx
Spartican Army g, 110, 111
Sportsmen g, 96
Stamp Act, The, 18
"Street Arabs", 53
Sullivan Law, 57
Swamp Angels g, 33

Tammany Hall, 34
Tchin Len, 61
"Territorial rights", 96, 135, *See* "Turf"
Thompson, Hunter, 92
Tom Lee, 59, 60
Tombs Prison (N.Y.C.) 26, 33
tongs, 58-61
tong war, 60-61
True Blue Americans g, 27, 31
"Turf", 28, 86, 124, 135, 138

University of the Streets, 114, 115, 121

La Vieja, 86
Vincent Astor Foundation, 112, 114
Violent crimes, 30, 42, 50, 64, 73, 88-90, 126, 139
Volstead Act, The, 70, 74 *See* Prohibition, Eighteenth Amendment

Wah Kee gl, 58
War on Poverty, 110
Washington D.C., 116
Watts (area of Los Angeles, Calif.), 107
Weapons of gangs, 31, 50, 57, 60, 61, 72, 77, 94, 95, 130-135
West Side (N.Y.C.), 37
Whitey Lewis (Jacob Siedenshner), g, 63
Whyos g, 41, 50, 64
Wild One, The, (movie), 90, 92
Wong Get gl, 59
Wood, Mayor Fernando, 35

YOU, (Youth Organization United)
Young Lords g, 109
Youth agencies and boards; first, 95-97; philosophy of N.Y.C. Youth Board, 99, youth workers, 99, 100, 124
Youth Organizations United, 116, 117, 118, 121, 122
Youth workers, 99, 100, 124

Zelig, Big Jack (William Alberts) gl, 63, 64